THE BEGINNINGS OF
AMERICAN ENGLISH

THE UNIVERSITY OF CHICAGO PRESS
CHICAGO, ILLINOIS

—

THE BAKER & TAYLOR COMPANY
NEW YORK

THE CAMBRIDGE UNIVERSITY PRESS
LONDON

THE MARUZEN-KABUSHIKI-KAISHA
TOKYO, OSAKA, KYOTO, FUKUOKA, SENDAI

THE COMMERCIAL PRESS, LIMITED
SHANGHAI

THE BEGINNINGS OF
AMERICAN ENGLISH

✪

Essays and Comments

✪

EDITED BY

M. M. MATHEWS

THE UNIVERSITY OF CHICAGO PRESS
CHICAGO · ILLINOIS

TO

G. G. M.

Preface

THE expression "American English" is used in this work in its generally accepted sense of "that variety of English which is spoken in the United States of America." This form of English had its beginnings when the colonists and settlers began to adopt new terms and develop new senses of words, and, still later, it became more definite when the vernaculars of the various groups began to coalesce into one recognized form of language somewhat distinct from the English of the mother-country.

The true beginnings of American English, therefore, antedate by fully a century the earliest written comments on the modifications that had taken place in the language. In the first chapter of this book I have pointed out briefly the circumstances under which some of the early changes in this branch of the English language were made.

During the past few years I have come upon many articles, letters, and other compositions that bear directly upon the subject of American English. Some of these documents are inaccessible except to those who can consult them in large libraries. Acting upon a suggestion made to me several years ago by Sir William Craigie, I have brought together a few of the more interesting of these records, and have furnished them with such notes and explanations as, I trust, may prove helpful to those who have not had occasion to study the differences that exist, or have existed, between the English of the United States and that of "Old England," as the early colonists called it.

In presenting the material here dealt with I have endeavored to follow the originals with scrupulous care, even to the extent of reproducing mistakes in spelling, punctuation, etc. To some of the more obvious errors in the texts I have called attention at the places where they occur.

It is a pleasure to express here my appreciation to those who have aided me in the researches that have made this book possible. Sir William Craigie has given me the benefit of his kindly counsels and has enabled me to secure material and aid that would have otherwise been difficult for me to obtain. Mr. George Watson, with his accustomed generosity, has given me highly appreciated assistance, especially with the proofs. His long experience on the staff of the *Oxford English Dictionary* has enabled him to save me from numerous inaccuracies. Professor Atcheson L. Hench, of the University of Virginia, has also cheerfully aided me in connection with the long article from the *Virginia Literary Museum*. Without his help I would have been greatly handicapped in my efforts to include this material, because the *Museum* is so rare that it was not practicable to secure photostats.

The librarians of the universities of Harvard, Yale, Brown, Princeton, Virginia, and Chicago have with their usual courtesy assisted me in locating and securing material some of which has not been easy to find. To Miss Ver Nooy, reference librarian at the University of Chicago, and to her assistants, I am especially grateful.   M. M. M.

CHICAGO
June, 1931

Table of Contents

CHAPTER I

Some Preliminary Observations

WHEN the first colonists to settle in New England reached that winter-swept land they soon discovered that the vocabulary they brought over from England was not perfectly suited to their needs in the new environment. The Puritans, and those who came later, in the course of time altered and expanded their common stock of words in such ways as to facilitate intercourse and communication in the new land. It is not to be imagined, of course, that such changes and additions as were made in the common vocabulary were effected with the deliberate, purposeful intent of amending or improving the language.

In fact, the speech modifications came about in a perfectly simple, natural way. The colonists were in a new environment where they found much that was different from what they had been accustomed to before coming here. The vegetable and animal life, for example, presented features that were in some respects novel to the newcomers.

One of the chief articles of food among the Indians was corn. The colonists had not seen any grain just like this before, so they were somewhat puzzled to know what name to give it. For some reason they did not adopt the Indian name, whatever that was, nor did they at first employ the name *maize* which the Spaniards had already taken over from a native dialect in Cuba. Instead, the Puritans used the expression *Indian corn* and for some time they distinguished the corn in America from that in England by the terms *Indian corn* and *English corn*. They kept this distinction in speaking of the meal produced from corn and used the terms *Indian meal* and *English meal*. After a time, however, it was no longer necessary or desirable to keep up the distinctions; the single word *corn* came to mean in this country *Indian corn*, and *meal* has no distinguishing word used with it.

It is interesting to notice that although the colonists did not adopt the Indian name for corn they did take over the native word *hominy*, to denote corn broken up and prepared as food.

To a fairly large number of other things—vegetables, trees, etc.—the Puritans applied native names, and this practice on their part and the part of other settlers has resulted in the presence in our everyday speech of such words as *chinquapin, hickory, persimmon, Sequoia, squash.*

Many of the animals that the colonists found here they recognized and accordingly designated by familiar names, but a few were strange and sooner or later had such Indian names applied to them as *coon, moose, possum, skunk,* etc.

The fact is that so many Indian words were added to the English vocabulary by the first settlers that a much longer treatise than this one would be necessary to enumerate anything like all of them. And even if we should make an exhaustive list of all the words in modern English coming from the speech of the American Indians we would still not know the whole story, for it is quite clear from the early New England records that many Indian words that were at one time in common use among the settlers are now no longer current. In other words, while there are many expressions of Indian origin that found an acceptable place in our language a great many others did not. One class of words in which mortality was high is that composed of place-names. There are of course scores of beautiful, euphonious Indian place-names in everyday use among us, but hidden away in the old records there are many others neither beautiful nor euphonious that did not survive. The following are a few of these taken at random from a volume of the New England records: *Pagonchaumischaug*, *Kitackamuckqutt*, *Wayunckeke*, *Maushapogue*, *Mashipawog*.

Not only place-names of Indian origin but also many Indian words of other sorts have almost or entirely disappeared. There is, for example, the word *peag*, taken over in colonial times from the speech of the Massachusetts Indians and found frequently in the early records. It has so nearly disappeared from use that many people will no doubt appreciate being told that it denotes a kind of shell used for money in commerce between the settlers and the Indians. On the other hand, the Algonquin word *wampum* of almost identical meaning has maintained its popularity to the present day. *Netop* is a word of Indian origin that is no longer heard. It meant a friend or crony.

Nobody, so far as I know, has ever manifested the slightest ill will toward the Indian words in our speech. The early colonists and their successors who are ultimately responsible for the presence of these words in English were not doing anything unusual or exceptional in adopting Indian terms. Colonizers and explorers have usually seen fit to enrich their language by borrowings from the languages of the people with whom they come in contact. The presence in English of words like *bamboo, calico, gingham, pagoda, shawl,* reflect English contacts with India; *boomerang* and *kangaroo* are reminiscent of far-off Australia, while words like *banana, chimpanzee, zebra,* represent African contributions to English.

Among the New England colonists, however, an unusual situation existed, a situation such as has never existed in any other country to which English-speaking settlers have gone. It is well to look somewhat closely into this situation for it was in a measure responsible for linguistic changes in our American English which have in times past aroused energetic and often sarcastic comments from British critics.

The English people who first settled in New England came as a rule from the humbler walks of life in England. In the main they were people who did not have much formal school training. Of course one should not forget that among the colonists was a large proportion of educated ministers but there were not enough of these leading spirits to attend to all the religious and governmental duties incumbent upon the members of the communities that were established. Unusual and important functions frequently devolved upon men who in their homelands would never have been faced with such tasks. One important function in colonial days in New England was that of keeping records of the activities carried on through the various governing bodies which the colonists established. It is clear from an examination of these records that they were in many instances kept by men who were not used to the pen and who were only vaguely familiar with the technical requirements of their new positions.

Many of these first recorders had not been to school enough to know how to spell some very common words. Moreover, these scribes were accustomed in their daily life to use pronunciations and words that seldom if ever appeared in the writings of those sophisticated enough to strive for what they regarded as standard form.

The records left us by these early New England clerks and secretaries are therefore interesting for the light they shed on the speech actually used by common people in certain parts of England during the first half of the seventeenth century. In England records of the kind kept in New England were made by people trained to write as they should speak, not as they really did speak. Consequently, the records kept in England do not possess the linguistic interest of those kept in New England at the same period.

The following spellings taken from a volume of the early New Haven records are instructive:

absenc	absence	privatly	privately
acrs	acres	repentanc	repentance
brest	breast	sariant	sergeant
cam	came	sentenc	sentence
chuse	choose	severly	severely
elc	else	shering	shearing
fenc	fence	sid	side
meddow	meadow	sinc	since
ordred	ordered	ther	there
pec	piece	wherin	wherein

These spellings show that in the early records the tendency was for unstressed vowels to disappear and for diphthongs to be reduced to simple vowels. It is not to be understood that these principles characterized all the spellings found in the records. They did not, but enough spellings showing these tendencies exist to make it quite clear that in the actual speech of the people the existence of the obscure vowels was not appreciated.

Nor are the New Haven records peculiar in exhibiting these tendencies. The spellings here given were taken from those records because it was in New Haven a century and a half later that there arose a noted lexicographer, Noah Webster, who drew down much wrath upon his head by proposing to spell certain words as they sound. His advocacy of such spellings as *ake*, *crum*, *iland*, *lether*, contributed substantially to his unpopularity with some of his countrymen.

Had the changes introduced by the colonists been limited to those indicated above not much would have come of them. But these scribes went further. They did not hesitate to put in their records any words they knew that expressed the idea involved.

One result of the scribal efforts of these early New England clerks is that in their records it is not unusual to find words and expressions that are not recorded in dictionaries. For example, the following expressions, though they occur frequently in the New England records, are not found, usually, in modern dictionaries: *coasting coat*, *corder* (one who cords wood), *corn basket*, *corn measure*, *corn room*, *corner post*, *country road*, *cross-fence*.

Again, by a careful reading of these New England

records it is not difficult to find expressions occurring earlier than lexicographers have shown them. In the following short list each word is followed first by the date of its earliest-known occurrence in the New England records and next by the date, in parentheses, of its earliest citation in the *Oxford English Dictionary*.[1]

cow yard, 1637 (1798)
creek (a stream), 1638 (1674)
crotch (of a road or river), 1698 (1767)
hob, [=hobnail], 1687 (1874)

hog reeve, 1637 (1759)
hoop pole, 1645 (1807)
horse bean, 1684 (1707)
horse cart, 1658 (1774)

These early scribes also adapted old words to new situations and used them with significations slightly different from those they had formerly possessed. For example, among the settlers it was customary to allot land to individuals and the old word *lot* came quite naturally to be used to denote each man's share. The word soon became quite common in this country, and hence the formation of such expressions as *to lot out*, to allot, and *lotters*, those appointed to do the *lotting-out*.

This tendency on the part of words in our language to take on in America slightly different meanings, and meanings in addition to those possessed in standard English use, has been quite marked. With us in the United States, for example, the word *fraternity* is often used to denote a Greek-letter society in a school or college. This sense of the term is distinctively American. What we call fraternities do not exist in England, and no occasion has arisen there for the word in this American sense. Similarly, with us the word *campus* is used more frequently than not to refer to

[1] Hereafter in referring to the *Oxford English Dictionary* the abbreviation *OED* will be used.

grounds around a school or college, but in England no need for the term in that sense has been felt.

Shut off as they were from any intimate association with other English people, and busy with the practical aspects of subduing the wilderness and establishing homes, the colonists naturally lost step with the changes going on in the language in Great Britain. Without thinking much about the matter they preserved in their speech words that for one reason or another had become obsolete in England.

The word *bug* illustrates this tendency. *Bug* at an early time in England was used somewhat loosely to mean an insect. It still has that meaning in the United States, but in modern British use it denotes a *bedbug, chinch*. Similarly the word *sick*, meaning ill, unwell, ailing, is largely restricted to the United States. In England the word *ill* is preferred.

It is doubtless clear from this brief notice of the activities of the early New England scribes that the records they made are of great importance for students of the histories of words. Up to the present time these records have not been fully utilized by lexicographers.

For over a hundred and fifty years the English language in America, progressing along the lines indicated above, had been deviating more and more from standards of acceptable use in England. During this century and a half great changes had taken place in the social and political life of the people who now styled themselves Americans. Settlers from various parts of Europe had swelled the population of the colonies. The Atlantic seaboard had become a meeting place of people speaking various languages. The

Dutch had settled around the mouth of the Hudson, and the English language profited by the addition to its resources of such words of Dutch origin as *boss*, *bowery*, *coleslaw*, *cookie*, *Santa Claus*, *sleigh*, *snoop*, *stoop* (n.), *waffle*. Settlers from Ireland, Scotland, Germany, France, and other countries had come and had contributed their share toward making American English differ somewhat from the English used beyond the Atlantic.

The fact should be borne in mind that the treatment given the English language in this country does not differ in kind from that given to the language wherever English colonists have gone. In India, Canada, Australia, and Africa the English language has been modified in very much the same way that it has in this country. With regard to the language in the United States two things should be borne in mind which have had a united influence in causing American English and British English to be contrasted.

The Revolutionary War caused the differences between Americans and Englishmen to be sharply accentuated. There was a tendency after the war for writers to single out and stress points of contrast between the peoples of the two countries. It was easy to be seen by the end of the eighteenth century that in details the language employed in the United States differed from that used in England. The Americans were quick to claim that the language as used by them was vastly superior to that employed in England, and the English lost no time in taking the opposite view of the matter. These two views have ever since been maintained with varying degrees of vigor by their adherents.

In the second place, among the colonies planted by England it has been only in the United States that a literature has been produced which can even remotely be thought of in comparison with that produced in the homeland. American authors and works have inevitably been compared with and contrasted with English writers and their products. These reviews and comparisons have tended to keep open the question of the relative superiority of the English used in the United States and that used in England.

The incessant bickerings about the merits of these two kinds of English have become somewhat tiresome. The differences that really exist between United States and British English have been so emphasized that enthusiastic partisans have thought these differences are sufficiently numerous and important to justify the use of the expression "American language" to designate the English employed in the United States. Mr. H. L. Mencken has written a valuable and readable book on the subject of *The American Language*.

The fact of the matter is of course that the English used in the United States and that used in England are so overwhelmingly alike that such differences as do exist hardly justify anyone in advancing a claim of superior excellence for either the so-called American language or the English language.

The really surprising thing about the English of England and that of the United States is not that they differ slightly, but that their difference is as slight as it is. When we consider the great number of people of different nationalities who have come to this country during the past three hundred years we may well marvel that the present-day speech is so nearly standard English that wherever an American travels in the English-speaking world he has no real difficulty in understanding the English speech he hears and in making himself understood.

The difference, however, between American English and British English has been an enticing subject for the past century and a half. Some of the observations made by those who have dealt with the subject are quite useless, and show that their authors were not competent to pass any judgment on any phase of the subject they treated. Other observations were made by people who had the background necessary to enable them to have sensible views about the growing divergence between British and American usage.

In the following pages there are brought together a few of the more interesting of these pronouncements on American English. The selections given are accompanied by explanatory comments that, I trust, may be welcomed by those who have had no occasion to direct their attention to any study of words, or to study American as contrasted with British usage.

The question of pronunciation is only occasionally gone into in commenting on the articles here reproduced. None of the writers herein quoted employed any phonetic transcript, and such spellings as they used have to be our guide as to how they pronounced. Ordinary respelling for indicating pronunciations is not a satisfactory system, and yet it is the only one employed by the observers whose comments are included in this book.

Pronunciation is a difficult, delicate matter anyway. Many people have an idea that there is one proper way of pronouncing practically all words, and that the dictionary is the place where this proper way may be found. A more nearly correct view of the matter is that there are various proper ways of pronouncing a large number of the words in our language. Many people are sensitive about pronunciations that they have been taught to believe are exclusively proper, and it is often painful to them to have their views on the subject called in question.

At the present time some English people are perturbed about the Americanisms in both vocabulary and pronunciations that are invading England by way of talking pictures. American actors and actresses are, meantime, doing their utmost to talk as they think English people talk. The results achieved are often interesting but never criminal. The fact is that pronunciation is not intrinsically one of the fundamentally important things in life.

CHAPTER II

Rev. John Witherspoon (1722-94)

BEFORE the middle of the eighteenth century the English used in the United States had been adversely commented upon by more than one critic. Francis Moore, who came to Georgia in 1735, included in his account of his voyage an uncomplimentary reference to American English. In describing the city of Savannah he wrote:

> When he was gone, I took a view of the town of Savannah. It is about a mile and a quarter in circumference; it stands upon the flat of a hill, the bank of the river (which they in barbarous English call a bluff) is steep and about forty-five foot perpendicular. . . . .[1]

A few years later, in the autumn of 1740, another newcomer to Georgia wrote a short account of the condition of that province. In his treatise the following sentence occurs:

> The Hill Country is very different, there being Marble, Chalk, Gravel, Rocks, and all the same Variety of Soil that is in Europe; with respect to the Proportion of the different Kinds of Soil, it cannot be given, unless the Whole were surveyed; but the American Dialect distinguishes Land into Pine, Oak and Hickery, Swamp, Savannah, and Marsh.[2]

So far as is now known, the first man to write at length about the differences between American and British English was John Witherspoon, a lineal

[1] *Collections of the Georgia Historical Society*, I, 94.
[2] *Colonial Records of Georgia*, IV, 670.

descendant of John Knox. He was born in Hadding-
tonshire, not far from Edinburgh, and having secured
an excellent classical education entered the ministry
of the Presbyterian church.

In 1766 the trustees of the College of New Jersey,
later known as Princeton University, invited Witherspoon to become president of that institution. At
first Witherspoon declined the offer, and it was not until two years later that he yielded to the solicitations
of the trustees and sailed for Philadelphia. He gave
the remaining twenty-six years of his life to Princeton,
which at the beginning of his tenure of office possessed
only one building besides the president's house. The
enrolment was less than one hundred and fifty when
Witherspoon and Professor Houston, assisted by two
tutors, constituted the faculty.

Witherspoon was not a very prolific writer, though
his works, collected and published in 1800–1801, fill
four substantial-sized volumes. In 1781 he contributed to the *Pennsylvania Journal and The Weekly
Advertiser*, published at Philadelphia, a series of papers known as the "The Druid." Numbers V, VI, and
VII of this series, appearing May 9, 16, 23, and 30,
1781, were devoted to a general discussion of language, and to an enumeration of such peculiarities of
American speech as had fallen under Witherspoon's
observation.

The three numbers of "The Druid" given below are
taken from the *Pennsylvania Journal*.

"THE DRUID," No. V

A man is not, even at this time, called or considered as a
scholar, unless he is acquainted in some degree with the ancient
languages, particularly the Greek and Latin. About 150 years

ago, however, those languages were better understood than they are at present; because, at that time, authors of reputation published almost all their works in Latin. Since the period above mentioned, the modern, or as they are sometimes called, the northern languages, have been gradually polished, and each nation has manifested a zeal for and an attention to the purity and perfection of its own tongue. This has been the case, particularly with respect to the French and English. The French language is as nearly as I can guess, about 50 years before the English in this respect; that is to say, it is so much longer since their men of letters applied themselves to the ascertaining, correcting and polishing of it. The English, however, has received great improvements within the last hundred years, and probably will continue to do so. He must have little judgment or great obstinacy who does not confess, that some late authors have written the English language with greater purity than those of the first character in former times. From this we may certainly infer, that the education must be very imperfect in any seminary where no care is taken to form the scholars to taste, propriety and accuracy, in that language which they must speak and write all their life afterwards.

To these reflections it may be added, that our situation in America is now, and in all probability will continue to be such, as to require peculiar attention upon this subject. The English language is spoken through all the United States. We are at a great distance from the island of Great-Britain, in which the standard of the language is as yet supposed to be found. Every state is equal to and independent of every other; and, I believe, none of them will agree, at least immediately, to receive laws from another in discourse, any more than in action. Time and accident must determine what turn affairs will take in this respect in future, whether we shall continue to consider the language of Great-Britain as the pattern upon which we are to form ours: or whether, in this new empire, some center of learning and politeness will not be found, which shall obtain influence and prescribe the rules of speech and writing to every other part.

While this point is yet unsettled, it has occurred to me to make some observations upon the present state of the English language in America, and to attempt a collection of some of the chief improprieties which prevail and might be easily corrected. I will premise one or two general remarks. The vulgar in America speak much better than the vulgar in Great-Britain, for a very obvious reason, viz. that being much more unsettled, and moving frequently from place to place, they are not so liable to local peculiarities either in accent or phraseology. There is a greater difference in dialect between one county and another in Britain, than there is between one state and another in America. I shall also admit, though with some hesitation, that gentlemen and scholars in Great-Britain speak as much with the vulgar, in common chit-chat, as persons of the same class do in America: But there is a remarkable difference in their public and solemn discourses. I have heard in this country, in the senate, at the bar, and from the pulpit, and see daily in dissertations from the press, errors in grammar, improprieties and vulgarisms, which hardly any person of the same class in point of rank and literature would have fallen into in Great-Britain. Curiosity led me to make a collection of these, which, as soon as it became large, convinced me that they were of very different kinds, and therefore must be reduced to a considerable number of classes, in order to their being treated with critical justice. These I now present to the public under the following heads, to each of which I will subjoin a short explication and a number of examples, with remarks where they seem necessary.

1. Americanisms, or ways of speaking peculiar to this country.

2. Vulgarisms in England and America.

3. Vulgarisms in America only.

4. Local phrases or terms.

5. Common blunders arising from ignorance.

6. Cant phrases.

7. Personal blunders.

8. Technical terms introduced into the language.

It will be proper to put the reader in mind, that he ought not to expect that the enumeration under each of these heads can be complete. This would have required a very long course of observation; and indeed is not necessary to my purpose, which is by specimens to enable every attentive and judicious per[s]on to make observations for himself.

1. The first class I call Americanisms, by which I understand an use of phrases or terms, or a construction of sentences, even among persons of rank and education, different from the use of the same terms or phrases, or the construction of similar sentences in Great-Britain. It does not follow, from a man's using these, that he is ignorant, or his discourse upon the whole inelegant; nay, it does not follow in every case, that the terms or phrases used are worse in themselves, but merely that they are of American and not of English growth. The word Americanism, which I have coined for the purpose, is exactly similar in its formation and signification to the word Scotticism. By the word Scotticism is understood any term or phrase, and indeed any thing either in construction, pronounciation or accentuation, that is peculiar to North-Britain. There are many instances in which the Scotch way is as good, and some in which every person who has the least taste as to the propriety or purity of a language in general, must confess that it is better than that of England, yet speakers and writers must conform to custom.

Scotland, or the northern part of Great-Britain, was once a separate independent kingdom, though, except in the Highlands, the people spoke the same language as in England; the inhabitants of the Lowlands, in both countries, having been originally the same. It is justly observed by Dr. Robertson, in his History of Scotland, that had they continued separate kingdoms so that there should have been a court and parliament at Edinburgh, to serve as a standard, the small differences in dialect and even in pronounciation would not have been considered as defects, and there would have been no more opprobrium attending the use of them in speech or writing, than there was in the use of the different dialects of the ancient Grecian republics. But by the removal of the court to London, and especially by the union of the two kingdoms, the Scottish manner of speaking, came to be considered as provincial barbarism; which, therefore, all scholars are now at the utmost pains to avoid. It is very probable that the reverse of this, or rather its counter part, will happen in America. Being entirely separated from Britain, we shall find some centre or standard of our own, and not be subject to the inhabitants of that island, either in receiving new ways of speaking or rejecting the old.

The examples follow.

1. 'The United States, or *either* of them.' This is so far from being a mark of ignorance, that it is used by many of the most able and accurate speakers and writers, yet it is not English. The United States are thirteen in number, but in English either does not signify one of many, but *one or the other* of two. I imagine *either* has become an adjective pronoun by being a sort of abbreviation of a sentence where it is used adverbially, *either the one or the other*. It is exactly the same with *ekateros* in Greek, and *alteruter* in Latin.

2. This is to *notify* the publick; or the people had not been *notified*. By this is meant *inform* and *informed*. In English we do not notify the person of the thing, but notify the thing to the person. In this instance there is certainly an impropriety, for *to notify* is just saying by a word of Latin, derivation, *to make known*. Now if you cannot say this is to make the public known, neither ought you to say this is to notify the public.

3. *Fellow countrymen*. This is a word of very frequent use in America. It has been heard in public orations from men of the first character, and may be daily seen in newspaper publications. It is an evident tautology, for the last word expresses fully the meaning of both. If you open any dictionary you will find the word countryman signifies one born in the same country. You may say fellow citizens, fellow soldiers, fellow subjects, fellow christians, but not *fellow countrymen*.

4. These things were ordered delivered to the army. The words *to be* are omitted. I am not certain whether this is a local expression or general in America.

5. I wish we could contrive it to Philadelphia. The words *to carry it, to have it carried*, or some such, are wanting. It is a defective construction; of which there are but too many that have already obtained in practice, in spite of all the remonstrances of men of letters.

6. We may *hope* the assistance of God. The word *for* or *to receive* is wanting. In this instance hope, which is a neuter verb,

is turned into an active verb, and not very properly as to the objective term assistance. It must be admitted, however, that in some old English poets, hope is sometimes used as an active verb, but it is contrary to modern practice.

7. I do not consider myself equal to this task. The word *as* is wanting. I am not certain whether this may not be an English vulgarism, for it is frequently used by the renowned author of Common Sense, who is an Englishman born; but he has so happy a talent of adopting the blunders of others, that nothing decisive can be inferred from his practice. It is, however, undoubtedly an Americanism, for it is used by authors greatly superior to him in every respect.

8. Neither to-day *or* to morrow. The proper construction is, either the one or the other, neither the one *nor* the other.

9. A *certain* Thomas Benson. The word certain, as used in English, is an indefinite, the name fixes it precisely, so that there is a kind of contradiction in the expression. In England they would say, a certain person called or supposed to be Thomas Benson.

10. Such bodies are *incident* to these evils. The evil is incident or ready to fall upon the person, the person liable or subject to the evil.

11. He is a very *clever* man. She is quite a *clever* woman. How often are these phrases to be heard in conversation? Their meaning, however, would certainly be mistaken when heard for the first time by one born in Britain. In these cases Americans generally mean by *clever*, only goodness of disposition, worthiness, integrity, without the least regard to capacity; nay, if I am not mistaken, it is frequently applied where there is an acknowledged simplicity or mediocrity of capacity. But in Britain, clever always means capacity, and may be joined either to a good or bad disposition. We say of a man, he is a clever man, a clever tradesman, a clever fellow, without any reflection upon his moral character, yet at the same time it carries no approbation of it. It is exceeding good English, and very common to say, He is a clever fellow, but I am sorry to say it, he is also a great rogue. When cleverness is applied primarily to conduct and not to the person, it generally carries in it the idea of art or chicanery not very

honourable; for example—Such a plan I confess was very clever, i.e. sly, artful, well contrived, but not very fair.

12. I was quite mad at him, he made me quite mad. In this instance mad is only a metaphor for angry. This is perhaps an English vulgarism, but it is not found in any accurate writer, nor used by any good speaker, unless when poets or brators [*sic*] use it as a strong figure, and to heighten the expression, say, he was mad with rage.

These shall suffice for the first class.

"THE DRUID," No. VI

I proceed now upon the plan laid down in my last paper, to the second general class of improprieties, viz. vulgarisms in England and America. Of these there is great plenty to be found every where in writing and in conversation. They need very little explication, and indeed would scarcely deserve to be mentioned in a discourse of this nature, were it not for the circumstance hinted at in the introduction, that scholars and public persons are at less pains to avoid them here than in Britain.

1. I will mention the vulgar abbreviations in general, as an't, can't, han't, don't, should'nt, would'nt, could'nt, &c. Great pains were taken by the Spectator to shew the barbarity and inelegance of that manner of speaking and writing. The endeavours of that author, and others of later date, have been successful in Britain, and have banished all such harsh and mutilated phrases from public speaking, so that they remain only in conversation, and not even in that among persons of judgment and taste. I need hardly say how far this is from being the case in America.

2. I *know'd* him perfectly well, for I *knew* him.

3. I *see* him yesterday, or I *see* him last week, for I *saw* him. In Scotland, the vulgar say, I *seed* him last week.

4. *This here* report of *that there* committee. Some merchants, whom I could name, in the English Parliament, whose wealth and not merit raised them to that dignity, use this vulgarism very freely, and expose themselves to abundance of ridicule by so doing.

5. He was *drownded* in the Delaware. This so common, that

I have known a gentleman reading it in a book to a company, though it was printed *drowned*, read *drownded*.

6. She has got a new *gownd*. This and the former are vulgarisms in conversation only; but even there very improper and unbecoming for persons of education. In London you are sometimes asked if you will take a glass of *wind*, for wine. Of the same nature are an impertinent *fellar*, for *fellow; waller*, for *wallow; winder*, for window.

7. Some on'em, one on'em, many on'em. This, though frequent in the northern parts of England, and some parts of America, perhaps is rather local than general. This indeed may be the case with several others which have fallen under my observation.

8. It *lays* in Bucks county, for it *lies*, &c. This is not only a prevailing vulgarism in conversation, but has obtained in public speaking, and may be often seen in print. I am even of opinion that it has some chance of overcoming all the opposition made to it, and fully establishing itself by custom, which is the final arbiter in all such cases. Lowth, in his grammar, has been at much pains to correct it; yet, though that most excellent treatise has been in the hands of the public for many years, this word seems to gain instead of losing ground. The error arises from confounding the neuter verb to *ly* with the active verb to *lay*, which are very different in the present preterite and participle. The first of them is formed thus, ly, lay, lien or lain; the second, lay, laid, laid.

9. I *thinks* it will not be long before he come. This is a London vulgarism, and yet one of the grossest kind. To this confusion or disagreement of the person, may be added the disagreement of the number, giving a verb singular to a nominative plural, which is more frequent than the other, as, after all the *stories* that *has* been told, all the *reasons* that *has* been given.

10. Equally *as* well, and equally *as* good. This is frequent in conversation and public speaking. It is also to be found in some publications, of which it is needless to name the authors; but it is just as good English to say, the *most highest* mountain in America.

11. One of the most common vulgarisms or blunders in the

English language, is putting the preterite for the participle. This is taken particular notice of by Lowth, in his grammar, as after he had *fell* down, for *fallen;* and in the same manner, *rose,* for *risen; spoke,* for *spoken; wrote,* for *written; broke,* for *broken.* Some of these appear, as he observes, barba[r]ous to scholars; others we are so accustomed to, that they give little offence to the ear. Had not a gentleman *threw* out, the reasons of protest were *drew* up. These are offensive, but you may meet with similar errors even in good authors, such as I had *wrote,* I had *spoke,* the bone was *broke.* The best way to judge of this impropriety is to try it upon a word that has been seldom so misused, as for example, If you go the battle pe[r]haps you will be *slew.*

12. Just as you *rise* the hill—little or no bread-corn is *grown* in this country. These are similar corruptions arising from turning neuter into active or passive verbs. They are also, if I am not mistaken, am[o]ng the newest corruptions of the language, and much more common in England than America. The above two examples are taken from Cook's first voyage, by Hawkesworth, where some others of the same kind are to be found.

13. I *sat* out yesterday morning, for I set out. The verb set has no change of termination, the present preterite and participle being the same. I set out immediately, I set out three days sooner than he; after I had set out. The error lies in taking the preterite of the verb *sit,* and making use of it for the past time of the other—sit has three terminations, sit, sat, sitten.

14. He said *as how* it was his opinion. This absurd pleonasm is more common in Britain than in America.

The third class consists of vulgarisms in America only. This must be understood so far as I have been able to observe, and perhaps some of them are local. It will not be necessary either to make the examples on this head numerous, or to say much upon them, because the introduction of vulgarisms into writing or public discourses is the same, whe[t]her they are of one country or another.

1. I have not done it yet, but am just going to. This is an imperfect construction; it wants the words *do it.* Imperfect constructions are the blemish of the English language in general, and rather more frequent in this country than in England.

2. It is *partly all* gone, it is *mostly all* gone. This is an absurdity or barbarism, as well as a vulgarism.

3. This is the weapon with which he defends himself when he is *attacted*, for attacked; or according to the abbreviation, attack'd.

4. As I told Mr. ———, for as I told you. I hope Mr. ——— is well this morning—What is Mr. ———'s opinion upon this subject? This way of speaking to one who is present in the third person, and as if he were absent, is used in this country by way of respect. No such thing is done in Britain, except that to persons of very high rank, they say your Majesty, your Grace, your Lordship; yet even there the continuance of the discourse in the third person is not customary.

5. I have been *to* Philadelphia, for *at* or *in* Philadelphia; I have been *to* dinner, for I have dined.

6. Walk *in* the house, for *into* the house.

7. You *have no right* to pay it, where right is used for what logicians would call the correlative term obligation.

8. A *spell* of sickness, a long *spell*, a bad *spell*. Perhaps this word is borrowed from the sea dialect.

9. *Every* of these states, *every* of them, *every* of us; for *every one*. I believe the word every is used in this manner in some old English writers, and also in some old laws, but not in modern practice. The thing is also improper, because it should be every one to make it strictly a partitive and subject to the same construction, as some of them, part of them, many of them, &c. yet, it must be acknowledged, that there is no greater impropriety, if so great, in the vulgar construction of *every*, than in another expression very common in both countries, viz. *all of them*.

Having finished these two classes, I shall make a remark or two upon vulgarisms in general. Probably many will think and say, that it would be a piece of stiffness or affectation to avoid them wholly in conversation or common discourse. As to some of those which have been described above, perhaps this may be admitted; but as to the greatest part, it is certainly best to avoid them wholly, least we should fall into them inadvertently where they would be highly improper. If a gentleman will not imitate a peasant, male or female, in saying *if so be*, and *forsooth*, and many other such phrases, because he knows they are vulgarisms, why should he imitate them in saying *equally as good*, or I *see him yesterday*, but because he does not know or does not attend to the impropriety?

The reader is also desired to observe, that we are not by far so much in danger of the charge of affectation for what we omit saying, as for what we do say. When a man is fond of introducing hard words, or studies a nice or pompous diction, he brings himself immediately into contempt; but he may easily attain a cautious habit of avoiding low phrases or vulgar terms, without being at all liable to the imputation either of vanity or constraint.

I conclude with observing, that as bombast and empty swelling is the danger to which those are exposed who aim at sublimity, so low sentiments and vulgar terms are what those are most in danger of who aim at simplicity. Now, as it is my intention, in the course of these papers, to set a mark of reprobation upon every affected and fantastic mode of expression, and to recommend a pure, and, as it may be called, classic simplicity, it is the more necessary to guard the reader against that low and grovelling manner which is sometimes mistaken for it.

"THE DRUID," No. VII

The fourth class of improprieties consists of *local phrases* or *terms*. By these, I mean such vulgarisms as prevail in one part of a country and not in another. There is a much greater variety of these in Britain than in America. From the complete population of the country, multitudes of common people never remove to any distance from where they were born and bred. Hence there are many characteristic distinctions, not only in phraseology, but in accen[t], dress, manners, &c. not only between one county and another, but between different cities of the same county. There is a county in the North of England, very few of the natives of which can pronounce the letter r, as it is generally pronounced in the other parts of the kingdom.

But if there is a much greater number of local vulgarisms in Britain than America, there is also, for this very reason, much less danger of their being used by gentlemen or scholars. It is indeed implied in the very nature of the thing, that a local phrase will not be used by any but the inhabitants or natives of that part of the country where it prevails. However, I am of opinion, that even local vulgarisms find admission into the discourse of people of better rank more easily here than in Europe.

1. He *improved* the horse for ten days. This is used in some parts of New England for riding the horse.

2. *Raw salad* is used in the South for *salad*. N B. There is no salad boiled.

3. *Chunks*, that is brands, half burnt wood. This is customary in the middle colonies.

4. He is *considerable* of a surveyor, *considerable* of it may be found in that country. This manner of speaking prevails in the northern parts.

5. He will *once in a while*, i.e. *sometimes*, get drunk. The middle states.

6. Shall I have *occasion*, i.e. *opportunity*, to go over the ferry. New England.

7. *Tot* is used for *carry*, in some of the southern states.

The fifth class of improprieties may be called *common blunders through ignorance*. In this they differ from the former classes, that the similarity of one word to another, in pronounciation or derivation, makes ignorant people confound them and use them promiscuously, or sometimes even convert them and use them each in the other's room. The following are examples.

1. *Eminent*, for *imminent*. How often do we hear that a man was in eminent danger.

2. *Ingenious*, for *ingenuous*. How common is it to say he is an ingenious young man—he is a young man of a very ingenious disposition. They are both English words. Ingenious signifies of good capacity; ingenuous signifies simple, upright, sincere[.] Ingenuity, however, the word that seems to be derived from ingenuous, is used in both senses, sometimes for fairness, openness, candor, sometimes for capacity or acuteness of invention. I should think this last, though done by good authors, to be contrary to the analogy of the language, especially as we have two words for these opposite ideas regularly derived from the correspondent adjectives ingeniousness and ingenuousness.

3. Three or four times *successfully*, for *successively*. This is a

blunder through ignorance, very common among the lower sort of people in England.

4. *Intelligible*, for *intelligent*. It was a very intelligible person who told me.

5. *Confisticate*, for *confiscate*. The most ignorant of the vulgar only use this phrase.

6. *Fictious*, for *fictitious*. That is no more than a *fictious* story. This is used by people somewhat superior to those who would use the former.

7. *Veracity*, for *credibility*. This is not a blunder in conversation only, but in speaking and writing. I have some doubt of the veracity of this fact, says a certain author. Veracity is the character of the person, truth or credibility of the story told. The same is the case with all or most of the words of similar formation, capacity, rapacity, tenacity. These all are applied to the person or the disposition, not to a particular action of the one or effect of the other. We say a man of capacity—this work is a proof of capacity, but not the capacity of this performance, and so of the rest.

8. *Susceptive*, for *susceptible*. I must acquaint the reader, that after I had marked this word as an example of the mistakes men fall into from ignorance, I found it in some English writers, who cannot be called altogether contemptible, and also in Johnson's dictionary. As to the last of these, I shall have occasion to make a remark or two upon that lexicographer under the next class, and therefore shall say nothing of it now. As to the other particular, I observe, that though the word is used by some writers, it is not only contrary to general practice, but contrary to the analogy of the tongue. All the adjectives ending in *ive* are of an active, and those ending in *able* or *ible* of a passive nature, as active, decisive, communicative, significative, demonstrative, and on the contrary, able, capable, communicable, demonstrable, contemptible.

9. They are so very *duplicit* that I am afraid they will *rescind* from what they have done. Here are two errors in one sentence. *Duplicit* is an adjective made by guess from duplicity, and *rescind* is mistaken, by the likeness of sound, for *recede*.

10. *Detect*, for *dissect*. A lady, in a certain place at dinner,

asked a gentleman if he would be so good as detect that piece of meat for her. To these I might add a long list of errors, in which ignorance of orthography makes a vitious pronounciation, and that pronounciation continued by the same ignorance, makes a vulgar word in place of the true one, of which take one example —A gentleman writes to his friend that on such a day they had a smart *scrimitch*, for *skirmish*.

"THE DRUID," No. VII

[Continued from our last]

The sixth class consists of *cant* phrases, introduced into public speaking or composition. The meaning of *cant* phrases is pretty well known, having been fully explained as long ago as the days of Mr. Addison. They rise occasionally, sometimes perhaps, from the happy or singular application of a metaphor or allusion, which is therefore repeated and gets into general use, sometimes from the whim or caprice of particular persons in coining a term. They are in their nature temporary and sometimes local. Thus, it is often said, a man is *taken in*, he is *bilked*, he is *bit*, that was a hit indeed, that is not *the thing*, it was quite *the thing*. Innumerable others will occur to every reader. Sometimes the cant consists in the frequent and unnecessary repetition or improper application of a word that is otherwise unexceptionable. Thus, when *vast* was in repute, a thing was vastly good and vastly bad, vastly pretty and vastly ugly, vastly great and vastly little.

It is worth while, in remarking on the state of the language, to reflect a little on the attack made by Addison, Steele, Swift, Pope and Arbuthnot, on many of these cant phrases in their day, such as bite, bamboozle, pos. rep. mob, &c. Some of them they succeeded in banishing from, or rather prevented from being ever admitted into public discourses and elegant writing, such as bite, bamboozle, &c. some they banished from all polite conversation, such as pos. rep. plenipo. and some have kept their ground, have been admitted into the language, and are freely and gravely used by authors of the first rank, such as *mob*. This was at first a cant abbreviation of *mobile vulgus*, and as such condemned by the great men above mentioned; but time has now stamped it with authority, the memory of its derivation is lost, and when a historian says an unruly *mob* was assembled in the streets, or he was torn in pieces by the *mob*, no idea of any thing low or ludicrous is conveyed to the mind of the reader.

I promised, under this head, to make a remark upon Johnson's Dictionary. It is a book of very great value on several accounts, yet it may lead ignorant persons into many mistakes. He has collected every word, good or bad, that was ever used by any English writer; and though he has, in the larger Dictionary, given his authorities in full, yet that is not sufficient to distinguish them. There are instances in which this may be the very cause of wrong judgment. If an author of reputation has committed a single error, his authority should not be made use of to sanctify that error—sometimes, also, the authors design is mistaken. In the abridgement of that Dictionary, at the word *bamboozle*, you find added, a *low word;* but the authority is *Arbuthnot:* now would not any man imagine, who was not otherwise informed, that Arbuthnot was a low writer; whereas, in fact, he used that word only to disgrace and put it out of practice. The lexicographer would have acted more wisely not to have mentioned the word at all.

It would be very easy to make a large collection of cant or low phrases at present in use, such as helter skelter, topsy turvy, upside down, the Devil to pay, at sixes and sevens, put to his trumps, flung all in a heap. Every one of these has been seen in print, and many others of the same stamp, as well as heard in conversation.

It is not long since I read, in a piece published by a sensible writer in this city, 'low methods of *shamming Abraham.*' Now, pray what is shamming Abraham? With some difficulty I have understood, that it is a cant phrase among seamen, for pretending sickness when they are well, and other fetches of the same kind. I should be glad to know how a foreigner could translate this expression into his own language.

Under the head of cant phrases I would include all proverbial or common sayings introduced into the language, as well as trite and beaten allusions. Of the first sort are these, I want to put the saddle upon the right horse, the labouring oar lies upon you;

of the second, the following, that is only *gratis dutum*, the supreme being by his almighty *fiat*, I will not pay any regard to *his ipse dixit*. All these are taken from printed pieces, some of them by authors not contemptible; the last of them, *his ipse dixit*, is of most frequent use, and yet is the most pedantic and puerile of the whole. I conclude with observing, that a cant phrase, if it do not dy by the way, has three stages in its progress. It is, first, a cant phrase; secondly, a vulgarism; thirdly, an idiom of the language. Some expire in one or other of the two first stages; but if they outlive these, they are established for ever. I have given an example of this above, in the word *mob*, and I think *topsy turvy* and *upside down* have very nearly attained the same previlege.

The seventh class consists of *personal blunders*, that is to say, effects of ignorance and want of precision in an author, which are properly his own and not reducible to any of the heads above mentioned. I shall give an example or two of this kind, because it will make the meaning of the former classes more clear. The examples follow.

1. 'The members of a popular government should be continually *availed* of the situation and condition of every part.' The author of this did not know that avail is neither an active nor passive, but a reciprocal verb; a man is said to *avail himself of* any thing, but not *to avail* others or *be availed* by them.

2. 'A degree of dissentions and oppositions under some circumstances, and a political lethargy under others, *impend* certain ruin to a free state.' Here a neuter verb is made an active one. I have before given some examples in which this is done commonly, but in the present case it belongs to this author alone.

3. 'I should have let your performance sink into *silent disdain*.' A performance may fall into contempt, or sink into oblivion, or be treated with disdain, but to make it sink into *silent disdain* is a very crude expression indeed.

4. He is a man of most *accomplished* ab[i]lities. A man may be said to be of distinguished abilities or great accomplishments, but *accomplished abilities* is wholly new.

5. 'I have a *total* objection against this measure.' I suppose the gentleman meant, that he objected to the whole and every

part of it. It was only an irregular marriage of the adjective to the wrong substantive.

6. An *axiom* as well established as any Euclid ever demonstrated. Now it happens, that Euclid, notwith[standing] his great love of demonstration, never demonstrated axioms but took them for granted.

I hope the reader will forgive me for not referring to the treatises from which these examples are taken. They were in general anonymous, and as it is probable many of the authors are alive, and may be of further use to their country, so being wholly unknown to me, without the least degree of envy or malevolence, I mean not to injure but improve them.

There remains only one class of improprieties to be illustrated, which, with some general remarks upon the whole, and an enquiry into the way in which the standard of a language comes to be fixed, shall be the subject of the next paper.

CHAPTER III

Four Additional Commentators

WE SEE (p. 17) that Witherspoon claimed
the word *Americanism* as his own invention. He was no doubt entitled to the credit,
for no use of the term earlier than his has been found.
It is a word which we shall have occasion to use frequently in the following pages, and on that account
we should adopt a suitable definition for it. Witherspoon's definition is not altogether satisfactory, for it
implies that once a term or construction, originating
in America, passes over into general use wherever the
English language is employed, it ceases to be an
Americanism.

The definition found in Webster's *New Interna-
tional Dictionary* is, for our purposes, open to the
same objection. That work defines an Americanism
as "a word or phrase peculiar to the United States."
The point is that the word or phrase may at first be
peculiar to the United States, but may later become
the common property of anyone who uses English.
On the whole, the definition given in the *OED* is the
one best adapted to our needs in the following discus-
sions. The *OED* defines an Americanism as "a word
or phrase peculiar to, or extending from, the United
States." This definition will permit us to claim words
like *lengthy* and *bread-stuff* as Americanisms, although both of them have long since ceased to be
"peculiar" to the United States, where, according to

the best information at present available, they both originated.

How can one tell whether a word or phrase originated in the United States? In the case of a great many words one cannot tell positively. The best dictionary to consult for determining the origin of a word is the *OED*, in which an effort is made to trace the life-history of every word that has existed in the English language from *ca.* A.D. 1150 to modern times. This great dictionary in ten volumes gives under the words which it contains examples of their early uses, and one can often without much difficulty tell from the evidence presented, even if the fact is not there specified, whether or not a word came into use first in the United States.

It is always wise, however, to remember that no dictionary can possibly contain all the words in our language. And, since dictionaries are of human origin, the best of them may contain mistakes. It often happens that the most one can say about the origin of a given word or expression is that the evidence so far available indicates that the term is or is not an Americanism.

Some of the words cited by Witherspoon may be regarded as Americanisms, but most of them are not. *Tot* (tote), for example, is usually regarded as an Americanism, though its origin is not known. The theory that it is an Africanism and reached this country by means of negro slaves has not been proved. The word is still in colloquial use. *Chunk* is no doubt a word of frequent occurrence in English dialect use. The *OED* records it in practically this same sense. It is often used at the present time. *Clever*, meaning

good-natured, agreeable, is usually regarded as typically American, and *considerable*, used as Witherspoon points out, may have in the United States first
taken on the meaning given. The expression *once in
a while* has no American flavor about it, but the
citation of it in the *OED* is for 1877, nearly a century
later than Witherspoon's notice of it. *Shamming
Abraham* also is not in any way typically American.
The examples of faulty constructions and pronunciations which Witherspoon cites need not detain us
here.

The readers of the *Pennsylvania Journal* must have
been interested in Witherspoon's observations on
American speech, for at least two of them wrote
letters to the *Journal* on the subject of the Druid
papers. The following communication appeared in
the *Journal* for June 20, 1781:

TO THE DRUID

The improprieties and peculiarities of expression, upon which
you have made remarks, have led my thoughts to the following,
which do not infrequently occur.

Manured, for inured.

Bony fidely, for bona fide.

Scant-baked, *slack-baked*, deficient in understanding.

Sarten, certainly.

Nice, handsome. I have frequently heard a beautiful woman
described by "she is a right nice crittur" (creature) "sarten."

E'en amost, e'en just, for almost.

Tarnal, for eternal.

Grand, for excellent. A *grand* farm. "Boots are *grand* things
to ride in."

Ou and *ow* are in many places pronounced like *eou*, as *keount*
for count, *keow* for cow.

In New England prophane swearing (and every thing *"similar* *to the like* of that"*) is so far from polite as to be criminal; and many of the lower class of people use, instead of it, what I suppose they deem *justifiable substitutions*, such as *darn* it, for d—n it.

I once heard a man say, another "swore terribly; he swore *e'en amost like a wood pile.*"

Power is often used to supply the place of a noun of *multitude*, as "a power of folks," for a multitude of people.

Many others might be added to the list, but they would protract it to an improper length. I cannot, however, conclude without giving you a speech, said to have been made by a member of an important public body, soon after the evacuation of Ticonderoga:—"General *Clear* behaved with great *turpitude* at the *vacation* of *Ty;* Gen. Burgoyne shot *language* at our people, thinking thereby to *intimate* them; but it only served to *astimate* them, for they took up the very *dientical language*, and shot it back again at the *innimy*, and did great *persecution;* for their wounds *purified* immediately."

X.

* *An expression I have heard in this city.*

It may help us in our effort to appreciate certain features of American English to notice with some care a few of the expressions mentioned by this contributor who signed himself X.

Manured for inured has now so completely disappeared from use that one might at first glance be inclined to suspect X of having blundered somehow. There is recorded, however, in the *OED* an obsolete use of the verb *manure* in the sense of "to cultivate, train (the body or mind, etc.)." Though the dictionary does not furnish just the evidence needed, it is not difficult to see how a "trained" person might be regarded as one inured to dangers, hardships, etc., and how the form *manured* might thus come to mean inured.

Scant-baked and *slack-baked* as expressions indicative of a deficiency in understanding are interesting. *Scant-baked* has never made its way into the dictionaries; while *slack-baked* in the *OED* is found only in quotations from 1823 onward, but the earliest date for the expression in a figurative sense approaching in meaning the one here found is 1882. In these two words, then, we have first an example of a word which was probably in common colloquial use at one time but failed to find a place in a dictionary, and next an instance of another word not fully dealt with in any dictionary. We must not conclude from the absence of evidence that these words were Americanisms. We can only say they possibly were first used in this country. Both have been largely superseded by *half-baked*.

Nice in the sense of handsome is a word common in English dialect usage, but I have never heard it so used in the United States. Several years ago while attending St. Giles Fair in Oxford I was watching a handsome female acrobat do some graceful poses. A countryman standing by me said in tones of admiration, "Ain't she nice?" The word has existed in English dialect use for a long time and is duly recorded in Professor Wright's *English Dialect Dictionary*.

Grand for excellent is not noted in the *OED* until 1816, and then from an American source.

Power in the sense of a large number, a multitude, is typical of many words once in reputable use that have now disappeared from our literary vocabulary. *Power* goes back to the middle of the seventeenth century, at which time it was quite respectable. It may still be heard in American dialect usage.

The pronunciations to which X called attention

may be dismissed briefly. Forms like *sarten, tarnal,* show the persistency, especially in dialects, of a pronunciation that is now usually condemned, though a number of words like *clerk, derby,* etc., are pronounced in English speech with an -*ar*-, and even in the United States we would not think of pronouncing "sergeant" any other way than *sarjent.* This pronunciation and that of *ou* and *ow,* which X mentioned, are fully dealt with by Professor Krapp in *The English Language in America,* II, 166 ff. and 207 ff.

The notice we have taken of a few words mentioned by Witherspoon and X, whoever he was, has shown (1) that no dictionary contains all the words that have at one time or another existed in our language; (2) that earlier evidence for certain words is constantly being found; (3) that common words like *clever* and *considerable* in passing through the crucible of American usage have often taken on meanings that are different from those which these words have in standard English use; and (4) that in this country old meanings of certain words sometimes remained long after they had disappeared in England.

We are now able to see somewhat more clearly why it is difficult to say of any given word that it is or is not an Americanism. The mere fact that the earliest evidence in the *OED* for a word is American may mean that the word is actually an Americanism, or it may mean nothing of the sort. The earliest passage, for example, containing the word *clever* in its American sense of good-natured, well-disposed, amiable, quoted by the *OED* is from Goldsmith's *She Stoops To Conquer.* The only evidence given in the *OED,* however, for *cloak,* in the sense of a cloak-like covering, is from

Emerson. Yet we should not hesitate to call *clever* an Americanism and *cloak* not an Americanism.

Though Witherspoon's comments on Americanisms were very mild, they aroused at least one reader of the *Journal* to write critically of the English used by the professor himself. The following letter appeared in the June 30, 1781, issue of the *Pennsylvania Journal*.

TO THE DRUID

As you appear to be sensible of the importance of a strict attention to grammatical propriety in speaking and writing, I am confident you will have no objections against being informed of any inaccuracies which may have escaped from your own pen: I shall, therefore, take the liberty of pointing out a few.

In No. 2, is this expression: "On these occasions he used to yoke them *in* his chariot, and make them draw him, in place of horses, to the temple." Should it not have been *to* his chariot? because we commonly suppose the *rider* to be *in* it.

"And make them draw him, *in place of horses*, to the Temple." *In place* is a *scotticism;* an Englishman would have said *instead* of horses. The *situation* of this phrase in the sentence appears to me to be improper; because as *him* is the immediate antecedent, it may be supposed to be what *in place of horses* refers to, (which I apprehend was not your intention) and may occasion such a mistake as the man made, who, reading "and he spake to his sons, saying, saddle me the ass: and they saddled *him*," unfortunately laid the emphasis upon *him*. The sentence, as I propose to correct it, will be—on these occasions he used to yoke them *to* his chariot, and make them, *instead* of horses, draw him to the Temple.

"This [bringing the 'Indian tribes upon the back settlements'] I call an act of extreme and unjustifiable barbarity, because their manner of making war is well known." Is not an *improper reason* assigned here? It is *their manner of making war*, and not its *being well known*, in which the barbarity of bringing them upon the settlements consists. The settlements in America were begun to be made near the ocean, and were gradually advanced into the country; for this reason I would prefer *frontier* to *back* settlements: nevertheless the settlements may be either the one or the other according to circumstances:—the following example will explain my meaning. A gentleman in London asked a print-seller's clerk if Mr. Sayer was at home? the clerk replied "yes, Sir, he is backwards"—"*backwards*, Sir, (said the gentleman) which way is that?" "*Straight forwards*, Sir, replied the clerk." This was literally true, for Mr. Sayer was then in the *back* part of the house, towards which the gentleman's *face* was turned. In like manner the settlements may be spoken of as being either *back* or *frontier*, according to circumstances; nevertheless, I would prefer the latter appellation, in the case before us, for the reason which I have assigned above.

In several instances the word *only* is misplaced, and injures the sense; as

In No. 2. "That destruction *can only fall upon* a few individuals," for can fall upon *only a few* individuals.

No. 4. "The poor man *only meant* to say, "for meaned to *say only*." [In this instance the participle *meant* is used for the preterite *meaned*.] These ignorant persons *only wanted* the opportunity," for *wanted only* the opportunity.

In No. 4. we see "indeed doctor says the lady." As a past transaction is refered to, *said* should have been used. Here I am reminded of an impropriety which occurs very often in conversation; I mean the frequent repetition of "*says I, says he,* and *says she*." I knew a gentleman who was remarkable for an attachment to these expletives, as well as for a fondness for polemical divinity:—in one of his theological disputations, he insisted that all men worshipped God from no other principle than self-love; and urged, in support of his thesis, that "the Devil was very sensible of this, for *says he*, will Job serve God for naught? *says the Devil, says he*."

But, to return from this digression;—

The following sentence, in No. 4, is incorrect. "An old gentleman, whom I knew, would often say in commendation of his son's wisdom, then a boy about ten years of age, &c." You certainly did not mean that his "*son's wisdom*" was a "*boy* about ten years of age," and yet the sentence is so formed as to admit of no other construction. Had you said, *in commendation of the wisdom of his son, then a boy,* &c. nobody could have been at a loss about knowing what was intended.

In No. 5. I find "some late authors have *written* the English language:"—here the participle *written* is used instead of the preterite *writ* or *wrote:*—it is proper to say a *book* is well *written.*

"No care is taken to form the scholars to taste, propriety and accuracy in that language which they must speak and write all their *life* afterwards." I apprehend it should be *lives,* as *scholars, they,* and *their* are plurals.

Although the use of *either* in "the United States *or either of them,*" is condemned by *Buchannan,* I think *Lowth* admits it to be proper; for he tells us that *"each, every, either* are called distributives, because they denote the persons or things that make up *a number* as taken *separately* or *singly.*" According to this, *either* may be applied to any component part of *the number* be it ever so large.

QUERCUS.

It would be interesting to know who this writer that signed himself Quercus was. His comments on Dr. Witherspoon's English show a pleasing combination of logical thinking and naïve humor. The expression *in place of* which he cited as a Scotticism is not labeled as such in the *OED,* and it is interesting to observe that the earliest citations in the *OED* which illustrate just this use of *in place of* are later than 1781 in date. Quercus had a notion, not uncommon in his day, that past participles like *written* could not properly be used in active constructions such as "I have written two letters," but were to be reserved for use in passive constructions such as "The book is well written."

Interest in the subject of American English was by no means confined to the readers of the *Pennsylvania Journal.* Throughout the eighteenth century there was in England and in the United States a decided tendency toward "improving" and "polishing" the language. This attitude is shown clearly in the two following extracts, the first of which is from a newspaper cutting inclosed in Governor Wentworth's dispatch from Portsmouth, New Hampshire, April 24, 1774, to the secretary of state for the colonies, and is found in the British Museum, Colonial Office Records, Class 5, Volume 938 (1772–74), page 186.

And as Language, is the foundation of science, & medium of communication among mankind, it demands our first attention, and ought to be cultivated with the greatest assiduity in every seminary of learning. The English language has been greatly improved in Britain within a century, but its highest perfection, with every other branch of human knowledge, is perhaps reserved for this Land of light and freedom. As the people through this extensive country will speak English, their advantages for polishing their language will be great, and vastly superior to what the people in England ever enjoyed.

I beg leave to propose a plan for perfecting the English language in America, thro' every future period of its existence; viz. That a society, for this purpose should be formed, consisting of members in each university and seminary, who shall be stiled, *Fellows of the American Society of Language:* That the society, when established, from time to time elect new members, & thereby be made perpetual. And that the society annually publish some observations upon the language and from year to year, correct, enrich and refine it, until perfection stops their progress and ends their labour.

I conceive that such a society might easily be established, and that great advantages would thereby accrue to science, and consequently America would make swifter advances to the summit of learning. It is perhaps impossible for us to form an idea of the perfection, the beauty, the grandeur, & sublimity, to which our language may arrive in the progress of time, passing through the improving tongues of our rising posterity; whose aspiring minds, fired by our example, and arbour [*sic*] for glory, may far surpass all the sons of science who have shone in past ages, & may light up the world with new ideas bright as the sun.

AMERICA, 1774   AN AMERICAN.

The following letter, which is given in full, needs no comment to make its meaning clear. I take it from *The Works of John Adams, Second President of the United States . . . . by His Grandson, Charles Francis Adams* (Boston, 1852), VII, 249 ff.

TO THE PRESIDENT OF CONGRESS

AMSTERDAM, 5 September, 1780

SIR,

As eloquence is cultivated with more care in free republics than in other governments, it has been found by constant experience that such republics have produced the greatest purity, copiousness, and perfection of language. It is not to be disputed that the form of government has an influence upon language, and language in its turn influences not only the form of government, but the temper, the sentiments, and manners of the people. The admirable models which have been transmitted through the world, and continued down to these days, so as to form an essential part of the education of mankind from generation to generation, by those two ancient towns, Athens and Rome, would be sufficient, without any other argument, to show the United States the importance to their liberty, prosperity, and glory, of an early attention to the subject of eloquence and language.

Most of the nations of Europe have thought it necessary to establish by public authority institutions for fixing and improving their proper languages. I need not mention the academies in France, Spain, and Italy, their learned labors, nor their great success. But it is very remarkable, that although many learned and ingenious men in England have from age to age projected similar institutions for correcting and improving the English tongue, yet the government have never found time to interpose in any manner; so that to this day there is no grammar nor dictionary extant of the English language which has the least public authority; and it is only very lately, that a tolerable dictionary has been published, even by a private person, and there is not yet a passable grammar enterprised by any individual.

The honor of forming the first public institution for refining, correcting, improving, and ascertaining the English language, I hope is reserved for congress; they have every motive that can possibly influence a public assembly to undertake it. It will have a happy effect upon the union of the States to have a public standard for all persons in every part of the continent to appeal to, both for the signification and pronunciation of the language. The constitutions of all the States in the Union are so democratical that eloquence will become the instrument for recommending men to their fellow-citizens, and the principal means of advancement through the various ranks and offices of society.

In the last century Latin, was the universal language of Europe. Correspondence among the learned, and indeed among merchants and men of business, and the conversation of strangers and travellers, was generally carried on in that dead language. In the present century, Latin has been generally laid aside, and French has been substituted in its place, but has not yet become universally established, and, according to present appearances, it is not probable that it will. English is destined to be in the next and succeeding centuries more generally the language of the world than Latin was in the last or French is in the present age. The reason of this is obvious, because the increasing population in America, and their universal connection and correspondence with all nations will, aided by the influence of England in the world, whether great or small, force their language into general use, in spite of all the obstacles that may be thrown in their way, if any such there should be.

It is not necessary to enlarge further, to show the motives which the people of America have to turn their thoughts early to this subject; they will naturally occur to congress in a much greater detail than I have time to hint at. I would therefore submit to the consideration of congress the expediency and policy of erecting by their authority a society under the name of "the

American Academy for refining, improving, and ascertaining the English Language." The authority of congress is necessary to give such a society reputation, influence, and authority through all the States and with other nations. The number of members of which it shall consist, the manner of appointing those members, whether each State shall have a certain number of members and the power of appointing them, or whether congress shall appoint them, whether after the first appointment the society itself shall fill up vacancies, these and other questions will easily be determined by congress.

It will be necessary that the society should have a library consisting of a complete collection of all writings concerning languages of every sort, ancient and modern. They must have some officers and some other expenses which will make some small funds indispensably necessary. Upon a recommendation from congress, there is no doubt but the legislature of every State in the confederation would readily pass a law making such a society a body politic, enable it to sue and be sued, and to hold an estate, real or personal, of a limited value in that State. I have the honor to submit these hints to the consideration of congress, and to be, &c.

JOHN ADAMS.

The dictionary "by a private person" which Adams mentioned was no doubt Samuel Johnson's two-volume work which appeared in 1755. It is worth noticing that Adams calls it a "tolerable" dictionary. It is now freely admitted that it really was a "tolerable" dictionary, but so great was the prestige and authority of Johnson that for a century after the appearance of his dictionary few people dared refer to that work as "tolerable." Noah Webster had no difficulty in provoking resentment when he not only said, in effect, that Johnson's dictionary was "tolerable" but also proceeded to make what he regarded as a better one.

CHAPTER IV

Noah Webster (1758-1843)

IT IS by no means an easy matter to deal adequately in a few pages with Noah Webster, the best-known lexicographer that America has produced. His writings on the subject of language would fill several books the size of this one, but there is not much of his that lends itself readily to reproduction in a small compass. Accordingly, we shall be content to give here only one letter of his. Before considering this letter, however, we may with advantage point out the circumstances under which it was written.

Noah Webster began his long and busy life in Hartford, Connecticut. He came of sturdy New England stock, being on his father's side a descendant of John Webster, a former governor of Connecticut, and being on his mother's side related to William Bradford, governor of the Plymouth colony. He graduated from Yale in 1778 and while pursuing the study of law engaged in school-teaching to help out with his expenses.

Just after the Revolution while Webster was teaching in the backwoods of New York he was impressed with the need of suitable textbooks for his pupils. The people he served were poor and books were scarce. Having in mind the needs of his countrymen, Webster set to work to compile his first text, *The American Spelling Book*, which was published in 1783. This thin little volume, a combination of primer,

reader, and spelling-book, went through many editions and revisions and became one of the most popular textbooks ever published. It has been estimated
that by 1865 nearly fifty million copies of this book
had been sold. Webster's "Old Blue-backed Speller,"
as it came to be known, maintained its popularity until
late in the nineteenth century.

Webster's interest in language and especially in
spelling became more profound as time passed. His
attitude toward the various phases of language study
which he engaged upon was that of a reformer. The
inconsistencies and absurdities of English spelling appealed to him as furnishing a fruitful field in which a
reformer might work. With a zeal which was not of
knowledge he proposed to change the spellings of certain words, and in his first dictionary, appearing in
1806, he advocated such spellings as *ake*, *crum*,
fether, *honor*, *iland*, *ile* (for *aisle*), *theater*, *wether*.

Webster's experience had, unfortunately for him,
not taught him that spelling and religion rank together as being subjects upon which people are sensitive. Since Webster's day many spelling reformers
have made their appearance among us, but it has not
been the fortune of any of them to increase the sum
total of their popularity by their willingness to lay
aside the revered spellings of their childhood. Reason
does not enter into this problem of spelling. The mere
fact that there is no linguistic reason for the *s* in
island means little or nothing to those of us who rejoice in spelling the word as we first learned to spell it.
Logic and common sense were on Webster's side in
most of his efforts to spell words as they sound, but
there are a few subjects, and spelling is one of them,

about which people refuse to be ruled by their intellects.

There was another direction in which Webster's industry led him into disgrace in the eyes of many of his contemporaries. In the course of his researches he had discovered that there were at least several thousand words not to be found in the best English dictionaries. Many of these words were old ones, and might therefore have been placed by Johnson in his dictionary of 1755 had not that worthy lexicographer, being only a human after all, failed to note and include them.

It disturbs some people to tell them they are using words not contained in the dictionary. Not every person who stands thus accused takes the attitude of the editor of the *Chicago Tribune* who in an editorial appearing in the *Sunday Tribune* for July 13, 1930, discussed the word *basically*. The editor having used this word, some reader favored him with the criticism that no dictionary at present contains *basically*, and asked the editor to define it. The editor admitted his surprise at not finding the word in the dictionaries he consulted, but insisted politely that it had been in use for some time and should be in the dictionary. The editor was quite right. *Basically* is at least thirty years old and should have been duly recorded in the editor's dictionary, as it has been in smaller works which the editor, apparently, neglected to examine.

The fact, of course, is that few of us think of turning to the dictionary before writing a sentence to see if all the words we propose to use are properly accredited in the language. We speak or write first and consult the dictionary later, if at all. The result of this natural and proper procedure is that most of us at times use a word that is not recorded in dictionaries. No American, I feel sure, would hesitate about using such a word as *Gideon* in referring to the order of traveling men that places Bibles in hotels, but neither *Gideon* in this use nor *Gideon Bible* is in the dictionaries I consult most often. The expression *Garrison duty* is in everyday use, but I have not found it in any dictionary. There are few people, let us hope, but that know what a *ginger-cake* is. The expression has been common in the United States for at least a hundred years, but it is not in the dictionary. *Tea-cart* is not in any dictionary I have examined but it is found in Sears Roebuck's *Catalogue*.

People who use such expressions as these do not feel the least uncomfortable until somebody comes along and tells them that they are using words not in the dictionary. There are some, like the *Tribune* editor, who even then do not get unhappy about the matter, but a great many people do, especially if such unwelcome tidings are delivered by someone whom they do not like anyway.

It is easy therefore to understand the extreme agitation many good people were thrown into by Webster's dictionary of 1806 in which he claimed to have added five thousand words "to the number found in the best English compends."

The reviewers lost no time in dealing harshly with the dictionary of 1806. Webster's sensible spellings were condemned and his five thousand additional words were branded as Americanisms or vulgarisms or some other undesirable kind of *isms*. Though Webster was blessed with an unusually thick skin, he winced under the flails of his reviewers. The letter which follows is one which he addressed from New Haven on August 5, 1809, to Thomas Dawes. It is given here as found in the *Monthly Anthology and Boston Review*, VII, 208 ff.

DEAR BROTHER,

I am charged with an attempt to innovate, by changing the orthography of words. To this charge I plead not guilty; for whatever my wishes may be, I yield them to the public sentiment. In the few instances in which I write words a little differently from the present usage, I do *not* innovate, but *reject innovation*. When I write *fether*, *lether*, and *mold*, I do nothing more than reduce the words to their original orthography, no other being used in our earliest English books. And when it is just as easy to be right as wrong, why will men object? I write *hainous*, because it is the true orthography from the French *haine*, *haineux;* and this was the manner of writing the word till within an age. The modern orthography is as vitious as it is perplexing. I write *cigar*, because it is an anglicized word from the Spanish *cigarro*. I write *melasses*, because it is the Italian *melassa*, from *mel*, honey, or the Greek *melas*, black. Is this innovation? When authorities are found on both sides of a question, the Lexicographer is at liberty to prefer that orthography which is most simple, or most etymological.

But when I see a difficult and unnatural orthography, which originated in mere mistake, and which converts a word into palpable nonsense, which is the case with the word *comptroller*, no consideration shall prevent me for correcting it in my own practice. Those who wish for an explanation of that word, will find it in the preface to my Compendious Dictionary.

But in the few alterations of this kind which I propose, I am guided by fixed principles of etymology, and endeavour only to call back the language to the purity of former times, supported by the authority of Newton, Camden, Lhuyd, Davenant, Pope, Thomson, Gregory, Edwards, and a host of other writers.

I do not write *publick*, *republick*, because the introduction of *k*, was originally, a useless innovation, wholly unknown to the primitive English, and because the prevailing practice in Great Britain and America, has revived the primitive etymological orthography, from *publicus*. I do not write *honour, candour, errour*, because they are neither French nor Latin. If we follow the French, the orthography ought to be *honeur, candeur, erreur;* if the Latin, as we ought, because they are Latin words, then we ought to write *honor*, &c. and this is now the best and most common usage.

In truth, there are some words whose orthography is unsettled, and the man who writes them in either manner for which he has authority, cannot be charged with deviating from any standard. This has ever been the case with the most eminent authors, and without a perfectly regular orthography, it must ever be the case.

But I am accused of introducing into my Dictionary *Americanism and vulgarisms*.

This is one of the most extraordinary charges which my opposers have ventured to suggest. I have indeed introduced into our vocabulary a few words, not used perhaps in Great Britain, or not in a like sense; such as *customable*, on the authority of a law of Massachusetts; *doomage*, on the authority of Dr. Belknap, and the laws of New-Hampshire; *fourfold*, as a verb, on the authority of the laws of Connecticut, and a century's usage; *decedent*, for deceased, on the authority of the laws of New-Jersey and Pennsylvania; and a few others, probably not twenty, noting them however as *local* terms. And is this an offense never to be forgiven? Such local terms exist, and will exist, in spite of lexicographers or critics. Is this *my* fault? And if local terms exist, why not explain them? Must they be left unexplained, because they are local? This very circumstance renders their insertion in a dictionary the more necessary; for as the faculty of Yale College have said in approbation of this part of my work, how are such words to be understood, without the aid of a dictionary?

But what have I done, that others have not done before me? Has not Johnson admitted *hog*, a sheep, and *tup*, a ram, upon the authority of local usage in England? Has he not inserted many such words? And why does *he* escape the censure of our fastidious American critics? So far is he from being censurable for this admission, that his works would have had more value, if he had taken more pains to collect and explain local terms.

But I have admitted one or two cant words, such as *caucus;* and what are Johnson's *fishefy, jackalent, jiggumbob* and *foutre!!* Let the admirers of Johnson's dictionary be a little more critical in comparing his vocabulary, and mine; and blush for their illiberal treatment of me! Instead of *increasing* the list of vulgar terms, I have *reduced* it, by expunging *two thirds* of such words inserted by Johnson!! Any person who will have the patience and the candor, to compare my dictionary with others, will find that there is not a vocabulary of the English language extant, so free from *local, vulgar,* and *obscene words* as mine! It was most injudicious in Johnson to select Shakspeare, as one of his principal authorities. Play-writers in describing low scenes and vulgar characters, use low language, language unfit for decent company; and their ribaldry has corrupted our speech, as well as the public morals. I have made it a main point to reject words belonging to writings of this character, and shall proceed as far as propriety requires, in cleansing the Augean stable.

I have rejected also a great number of words introduced by a species of pedantry very common a century ago; such as *adjugate, abstrude, balbucinate.* Of this species, and other words not legitimate, between two and three thousand will be rejected. On the other hand, I have enriched the vocabulary with such words as *absorbable, accompaniment, acidulous, achromatic, adhesiveness, adjutancy, admissibility, advisory, amendable, animalize, aneurismal, antithetical, appellor, appreciate, appreciation, arborescent, arborization, ascertainable, bailee, bailment, indorser, indorsee, prescriptive, imprescriptible, statement, insubordination, expenditure, subsidize,* and other elegant and scientific terms, now used by the best writers in Great Britain and America. The number of these is not exactly known; but of the terms now well authorized, Johnson's dictionary is deficient in five or six thousand words, or about a seventh part of the English vocabulary.

But I will trouble you and the public no farther. Enough has been said to satisfy the candid and liberal; and more would not satisfy men of a different character.

N. Webster.

The Hon. Thomas Dawes, Esq.

POSTSCRIPT

In the remarks prefixed to my letter in the Centinel of August 2, you mention that my omitting *a* in *read* (which by the way is a mistake) and in *breadth*, with a few similar peculiarities, has probably had an effect in limiting the circulation of my *Elements of Useful Knowledge.* This may be true in Boston; but it is not true in all parts of the country, for the work is extensively used. For retrenching the *a* in *bredth*, I have however *royal authority;* and Massachusetts gentlemen should be the last to complain of that correction of error, for it is the orthography of the word in the original charter of the Colony. Hazard. Col. I. 239, 240.

But I do not insist upon the correction. Men, who are fond of improvement, and desirous of correcting errors in everything else, seem determined that no errors shall be corrected in language. No blunder, no irregularity, no absurdity, however enormous, in writing, if it has obtained a general currency, must now be disturbed! Not even a barbarism of the fourteenth century must now be violated by the unhallowed hand of reformation! Such is the spirit of critics, but such is not the sense of the community, nine tenths of whom would rejoice at a thorough reformation.

When a plain unlettered man asks why words are so irregularly written, that the *letters are no guide to the pronunciation,* and the noblest invention of man loses half its value; we may silence, tho not convince him, by saying, that such is the old practice, and we must not deviate from the practice of our grand fathers even when they have erred! But when I see such blunders as *comptroller* and *island* palmed upon a nation by the merest ignorance, I confess for myself I cannot repress my desire to correct them, as they disgrace the learning and criticism of the nation. See the preface to my Compendious Dictionary. A few such blunders I shall attempt to correct. The legislature of Connecticut have seen fit to adopt the correct orthography of *controller*, in their statutes, and I trust the example will be followed by others. But my proposed corrections are few, and my orthography differs from that of the English, not more than English authors differ from each other. The truth is a reformation of orthography might be made with few changes, and upon a

plan so simple as not to require an hour's attention to be perfectly master of it; and it might be introduced in a tenth part
of the time required to render general the practice of reckoning
money by dollars and cents. But I shall not attempt it. If men
choose to be perplexed with difficulties in language, which ordinary men are never able to surmount, I will not contend with
them, by endeavoring to remove such difficulties against their
will.

N. W.

Webster acted upon the sentiment expressed in the
last lines of his postscript and abandoned many of the
spellings which he had insisted upon at the beginning
of his career as a lexicographer. The Websterian tradition in spelling has, however, been sufficiently strong
to cause noticeable differences to exist at the present
time between English and American spelling. In the
United States we spell *honor*, *theater*, *plow*, *traveled*,
traveler, *imperiled*, *skillful*, *wagon*, and a considerable
number of words orthographically akin to some of
these, in a manner slightly different from that preferred in British use.

Webster's efforts to "preserve the purity of the
language" were not, of course, condemned by all of his
contemporaries. The following is the first part of a
letter written to Webster by Benjamin Franklin, on
December 26, 1789.[1]

DEAR SIR,

I received some Time since your *Dissertations on the English
Language*. The Book was not accompanied by any Letter or
Message, informing me to whom I am obliged for it, but I suppose it is to yourself. It is an excellent Work, and will be greatly
useful in turning the Thoughts of our Countrymen to correct
Writing. Please to accept my Thanks for it as well as for the

[1] The entire letter is printed in *The Writings of Benjamin Franklin*, ed. A. H.
Smyth (New York, 1905–07), X, 75 ff.

great honour you have done me in its Dedication. I ought to have made this Acknowledgment sooner, but much Indisposition prevented me.

I cannot but applaud your Zeal for preserving the Purity of our Language, both in its Expressions and Pronunciation, and in correcting the popular Errors several of our States are continually falling into with respect to both. Give me leave to mention some of them, though possibly they may have already occurred to you. I wish, however, in some future Publication of yours, you would set a discountenancing Mark upon them. The first I remember is the word *improved*. When I left New England, in the year 23, this Word had never been used among us, as far as I know, but in the sense of *ameliorated* or *made better*, except once in a very old Book of Dr. Mather's, entitled *Remarkable Providences*. As that eminent Man wrote a very obscure Hand, I remember that when I read that Word in his Book, used instead of the Word *imployed*, I conjectured that it was an Error of the Printer, who had mistaken a too short *l* in the Writing for an *r*, and a *y* with too short a Tail for a *v*; whereby *imployed* was converted into *improved*.

But when I returned to Boston, in 1733, I found this Change had obtained Favour, and was then become common; for I met with it often in perusing the Newspapers, where it frequently made an Appearance rather ridiculous. Such, for Instance, as the Advertisement of a Country-House to be sold, which had been many years *improved* as a Tavern; and, in the Character of a deceased Country Gentleman, that he had been for more than 30 Years *improved* as a Justice-of-Peace. This Use of the Word *improved* is peculiar to New England, and not to be met with among any other Speakers of English, either on this or the other Side of the Water.

During my late Absence in France, I find that several other new Words have been introduced into our parliamentary Language; for Example, I find a Verb formed from the Substantive *Notice; I should not have* NOTICED *this, were it not that the Gentleman*, &c. Also another Verb from the Substantive *Advocate; The Gentleman who* ADVOCATES *or has* ADVOCATED *that Motion*, &c. Another from the Substantive *Progress*, the most awkward and abominable of the three; *The committee, having* PROGRESSED, *resolved to adjourn.* The Word *opposed,* tho' not a new Word, I find used in a new Manner, as, *The Gentlemen who are* OPPOSED *to this Measure; to which I have also myself always been* OPPOSED. If you should happen to be of my Opinion with respect to these Innovations, you will use your Authority in reprobating them.

We know enough about Webster's sentiments on the subject of words to justify us in feeling sure that he did not "happen to be of" Franklin's "opinion with respect to these innovations." The words *improve* (meaning employ), *notice* (v.), *advocate* (v.), *progress* (v.), *opposed* (ppl. a.), which Franklin hoped Webster would join him in "reprobating," appeared in the large two-volume edition of Webster's dictionary brought out in 1828—and they appeared with no "discountenancing mark" about them.

These words are interesting, however. With regard to the verb *notice* the *OED* says: "Not much used before the middle of the 18th cent., after which it becomes common in American use, and is also mentioned as a Scotticism." *Advocate* (v.), meaning to plead or raise one's voice in favor of, was just coming into use in Franklin's time; the earliest citation of it in the *OED* is for 1767. The verb *progress,* we learn from the *OED,* occurred during the sixteenth and seventeenth centuries, but although it became obsolete in England during the eighteenth century, it was either retained or formed anew in America. From America it was readopted into English use after 1800, but in the sense of go on, proceed, advance, it is still more used in America than in England. The participle *opposed* in the sense Franklin mentions was just coming into use in his day. His use of it is the earliest cited in the *OED.*

Franklin's ignorance of the word *improve* in the sense he mentions is interesting. *Improve* in the sense of employ is a very old word, dating back to at least the early part of the sixteenth century. It must have been in common use throughout New England before and during Franklin's time. The following illustrations of its use in New England are interesting:

1639. *Collections Connecticut Historical Society*, VI (1897), 11: Itis ordrd that the Townsmen haue liberty to Improue men for the killing of woolfs either by Hunting or shoting.

1664. *Records Colony of New Plymouth*, IV (1855), 58: The said Rushell was found blame worthy, in takeing vp of an axe, and indeauoring to improue it against the said Indians in a turbulent and dangerous manor.

1751. *Boston Records*, XVII (1887), 259: John Bish . . . . saith, that forty six years ago Mr. Thomas Hunt occupied & improved a Blacksmith's Shop then and now standing upon an old Wharffe.

1776. *New England Historical and Genealogical Register*, XXX (1876), 384. Mr. Adam Knox . . . . has been long improved in this Town as a Pilot.

Illustrations such as these lead one to suspect that if Franklin had not often heard the word *improve* used in the sense of employ he was about the only man in New England who had not.

CHAPTER V

David Humphreys (1752-1818)

THE man who compiled what is now known as the earliest glossary of Americanisms was David Humphreys, a native of Connecticut and a graduate of Yale. He rendered valuable military service to the American cause during the Revolution, and was esteemed highly by Washington, through whose influence he went abroad in 1784 as secretary to the commission appointed to negotiate commercial treaties with foreign powers. In 1790 he went to Portugal as America's first minister to that country. Later he served as minister plenipotentiary to Spain.

As early as 1786 Humphreys had gained some reputation as a writer. He was identified with the group known as the "Hartford Wits." Among his writings there are two dramas, *The Widow of Malabar* and *The Yankey in England*. In the back of the last-named play there is a Glossary, "Of words used in a peculiar sense, in this Drama." The word-list dates back to 1815, the year in which *The Yankey in England* was published.

This Glossary, containing about 275 expressions, has special interest in view of the fact that in writing the play in which the Glossary occurs Humphreys had in mind the delineation of three distinct types of American character. He explains how the representatives of these types vary from one another because of different educational attainments. In the play General Stuart and Admiral Dixon represent American college-bred men who have attained distinction. Mr. Newman belongs to the middle class, educationally speaking, his schooling having extended only through the grammar school. Doolittle, the "Yankey," represents the third class. What schooling Doolittle received was limited to the free public schools. Humphreys felt that this third type of American character, represented by Doolittle, was little known abroad.

It is somewhat surprising that Humphreys did not arrange his list of words in absolutely alphabetical order. Some words in the list are spelled differently from the way they appear in the play itself. For illustrating the use of some of the words I have felt justified in giving excerpts from the play. These I have placed in brackets. Humphreys placed at the beginning of his Glossary a paragraph of explanation:

GLOSSARY

Of words used in a peculiar sense, in this Drama; or pronounced with an accent or emphasis in certain districts, different from the modes generally followed by the inhabitants of the United States; including new-coined American, obsolete English, and low words in general.

A

Abord, for, on board.

Afeard, afraid.

Afore, before.

Agin, again.

Ant I, probably from, and I, used however rather as a negative. [I'm rather in a strait, jest now, and don't want to stan chaffering and stickling, ant I (p. 22).]

A-nuff, enough.

Argufying, arguing.

Arter, after.

Atarnal, eternal.

Atarnity, eternity.

Awful, ugly.

Ax, ask.

B

Ban't, } am, or as, or are not.
Ben't, }

Becaise, because.

Berrying, burying. [I'll du as the boys du, when they go by the berrying-yard alone, in a dark night (p. 77).]

Beleve, believe.

Bile, boil.

Bin, been.

Bissy, busy.

Bissness, business.

Blud, blood.

Boggling, difficulty, delaying, unnecessarily hesitating.

Boost, raise up, lift up, exalt.

Borrerd, borrowed.

Boot, *to boot*, something given into the bargain.

Bred-stuffs, all kinds of flour, meal, farinaceous substances, grain. In England, corn is used as the generic term. In America, corn is always intended to apply to maize—otherwise called Indian corn—the most abundant and useful vegetable production in the United States, from the extreme northern to the southern boundary.

Briled, broiled.

Brussels, bristles.

Buty, Beauty.

C

Calculate, used frequently in an improper sense, as reckon, guess.

Captivated, captured, taken prisoner.

Cent, 1-100th part of a dollar—a copper coin of the United States.

Clever, relating to moral character—not skilfulness or dexterity.

Chaffering, holding a long talk.

Chaunce, chance.

Chirk, churk, brisk, lively, in good spirits.

Chares, chores, trifling employments at or near home.

Cleverly, very well.

Close, clothes.

Clus, close.

Concarning, concerning.

Cood, could. [I cood form a more righter judgment of you (p. 43).]

Copper, formerly current money of the value of a halfpenny in England.

Count, (in provincial use,) estimate, reckon.

Cum, came.

Cumfort, comfort.

Curridge, courage.

Critturs, creatures.

Curious, extraordinary.

Cuss, curse.

Cussed, cursed.

Cute, acute, smart, sharp.

D

Darned, old English.

Darter, daughter.

Dasent, dare not.

Despud, desperate.

Despudly, desperately.

Dilly dallying, wasting time for little purpose.

Divil, devil.

Druv, driven.

Dreadful, used often as, very, excessively; even as it regards beauty, goodness, &c.

Du, do.

Dubble, double.

Duds, old clothes.

Dum, dumb.

Dumpish, heavy, silly.

Du pry tel, (exclamation probably from) do pray tell.

Duse, does.

E

Eend, end.

Enny, any. [I don't incline to be with enny one who has a *familiar*, or that has enny thing to du with the old sarpent (p. 49).]

Enny-wheres, any where.

E'en-a-most, almost.

Extrumpery, extempore.

F

Fairce, farce, fierce.

Fairm, farm, firm.

Farmament, firmament.

Fleering, } terms of contempt, vulgar.
Flouting, }

Flip, liquor made of rum, beer and sugar, with a hot poker put into the mug to stir it.

Flustration, extreme agitation.

Fokes, folks.

Forgit, forget.

Forrerd, forward.

Fort, fault. [Well, Mister, if you don't understand plain English, that is'nt my fort (p. 29).]

Fortin, fortune.

Fortino, fortizno, for aught I know.

Forzino, far as I know.

F'rall that, for all that, or notwith-
standing, &c.
Friggit, frigate.
Frolics, country festival sports.
Frind, friend.
Furder, farther.

G

Gals, girls.
Gawkey, awkward.
Gimcracks, (nice bagatelles) curious
trifles.
Gin, given, gave.
Gineral, *Gin'ral*, General.
Gineration, generation.
Glib, smooth, easy.
Gownd, gown.
Granny, grand-mother.
Guess, instead of being applied to
things conjectural, misapplied to
such as are past, present—certain;
believe, think.
Gum, foolish talk, nonsense. [I won't
hear nun of your gum (p. 34).]
Gumtion, sense, understanding, intel-
lect.

H

Han't, }
Havn't, } have not
Hansum, handsome.
Harty, well.
Hectored, bullied, insulted by domi-
neering.
Her'n, her own, hers.
Heerd, heard.
Hild, held.
Hoss, horse.
Huffy, ill-natured.
Hull, whole.
Hum, home.
Humbly, homely. [Well, well, I know
it now—hum is hum, be it ever so
humbly (pp. 19–20).]

I

Ile, oil.
Improve, employ, occupy. [I should be
glad to know, what kind of way
you count to improve me in (p.
29).]
Inyons, onions. [It is spelled *inions* on
p. 41.]

J

Jeerings, contemptuous sneers.
Jest, just.
Jeesting, jesting.
Jiffing, or *jiffin*, instantaneously.
Jumping jings, jingoes, expletives indi-
cative of confirmation.
Jurk, jerk.

K

Keow, cow. ['Tis well that cussed
keows have short horns, as the
proverb saies (p. 70).]
Ketch, catch.
Kill-dried, (the preparation of the meal
of maize or Indian corn for exporta-
tion,) kiln-dried.
Kittle, kettle.
Kiver, cover.
Knack, faculty of doing things with
facility.
Know'd, knew.

L

Larning, learning.
Leetle, little.
Lengthy, long. [I looked nation poorly
for a lengthy while arterwards (p.
42).]
Licker, liquor.
Lines, loins.
Lovyier, lover.
Lug, (very vulgar) bring, bring in, lift,
hand.

M

Mad, (not in the usual sense, insane,)
to make angry.
Mainly, mostly.
Mannerliness, good breeding, good
manners.
Marcy, mercy.
Massiful, merciful.
Mayn't, may not.
Meb-be, may be.
Munching, (low word,) chewing with
a mouth full.
Muggy, sultry, close air, very hot.

N

Naborly, neighbourly.
Nation, very extraordinarily. [—you

were a nation deal wiser than brother Jonathan (p. 19).]

Nationality, attachment to clan or country, belonging to, or fondness for a nation.

Native, (last syllable pronounced long,) native.

Neest, nest.

Nice, smart, tidy, spruce.

Nicely, in good health.

Nip, (original American,) pint, half pint bowl.

Notion, ⎤ used frequently not in the
Notions, ⎬ English sense of the
Notional, ⎦ words.

Nuther, neither.

Nick-nacks, trifling superfluous articles.

O

O, the Dickens, exclamation.

Obstropulous, obstreperous.

On't, on it, of it.

Ort, ought.

Outlandish, strange, foreign.

Overmatch, superior.

Owny towny, (*owny downy, ounty tounty*) peculiarly belonging to one. [—my owny, towny, Lydy Lovett, the Deacon's darlin darter (p. 19).]

P

Paerils, perils.

Parfect, perfect.

Parson, person.

Peek,   ⎤
Peeking, ⎬ to observe slily and sneak-
Peep,   ⎦ ingly.

Pertection, protection.

Pertest, protest.

Pestered, very excessively.

Plaguy, as a degree of comparison— very—to enhance the force of the word with which it is connected.

Poke your fun, jeer, pester, plague.

Potecary, Apothecary.

Poorly, miserably, ill.

Prehaps, perhaps.

Presarved, preserved.

Pritty, pretty.

Pluck, heart, courage, spirit.

Put out, disobliged, offended.

Q

Quarte, quart.

Quiddities, trifling niceties, odd behaviour.

Quiddles, disorder in the head, moping disease in horses, dizziness.

R

Railly, really.

Rather, (pronounced narrow on the first syllable) frequently used to diminish or qualify the term to which it is applied—sometimes pronounced *Ruth-er*.

Reckon, calculate, depend on the fact, sometimes nearly in the sense in which guess is misapplied.

Roiled, disturbed, applied to liquors and temper.

Rubbige, rubbish. [Good riddance to bad rubbidge (p. 88).]

Ruff, roof.

S

Saie, say.

Sabba-da, Sabbath-day.

Saisse, or *Sairse*, sauce. [—it has bin said by them of old time, "there is reason in roasting eggs," and that "what is sairse for the goose, is sairse for the gander" (p. 55).]

Saisy, saucy.

Sarpent, serpent.

Sarvice, service.

Sarvant, servant.

Sartinly, certainly.

Scart, scared.

Scholard, scholar. [*Schollard* on p. 79.]

Seed, saw.

Sen, since.

Sheep, ship.

Sha'n't, shall not.

Shabby,   ⎤ applied to ill looks or ap-
Shabbily, ⎦ pearance in dress, vulgar.

Shood, should.

Shugar, sugar.

Shute, shoot.

Shure, sure.

Sitch, such.

Slim, ⎤ used in a peculiar sense. [I
Slink, ⎦ feel pritty slim (p. 40).]

Snap, to break short.
Snappish, petulant, easily provoked.
Sneaking, used in a peculiar sense.
[I've a sneaking notion— (p. 102).]
Sparked it, (young men keeping company with young women and sitting by the fire after the family has gone to bed,) courting.
Spook, (a word used by the Low Dutch in some parts of America,) apparition, ghost, hobgoblin.
Spose, suppose.
Spry, acute, nimble.
Sperit, spirit.
Spunk, courage.
Staggers, horse-apoplexy, wild conduct, madness.
Stan, Stand.
Stickling, hesitating, delaying.
Stiddy, steady.
Strait, straight.
Stur, stir.
Stunded, stunned.
Stump, challenge. [I'll stump 'em all, ... (p. 102).]
Sumwheres, some where.
Swags, exclamation.
Swamp it, ridiculous kind of asseveration.
Swimmed, swam.
Swound, swoon.
Swap, Swop, exchange.
Suzz! Surs! a corruption from Sirs.

T

Tarms, terms.
Tarnation, used in a peculiar sense.
Tantrums, Tantarams, do.
Tatterations, do.
Tawking, talking.
Techy, easily irritated, froward.
Telled, told.
Toddy, (beverage) rum, sugar and water mixed together.

To-rights, immediately, instantly. [I'll be back, to-rights (p. 53).]
Trim, habiliments, dress.
Trade, physic, medicine.
Truck, to barter, exchange one thing for another.
Trampoosing, traversing.
Tuff, tough.
Twang, nasal pronunciation.
Twistical, tortuous, not above-board, not quite moral.
Twitted, reproached.

U

Underlin, an inferior animal.
Unpossible, impossible.
Uppish, (vulgarism) proud, arrogant.

V

Vacarme, (French) to make a noise, racket, scold.
Van, exclamation.
Vaggers, do.
Vartuous, virtuous.
Varmount, Vermont.
Varses, verses.
Vittles, victuals.
Venture, offer a bet, lay a wager, stake.
Vouch, vouch it, vouch on't, a species of asseveration.
Vow, do.
Vum, do.
Vumpers, do.
Viges, voyages.

W

Wage, or *wager*, to bet.
Wood, would.

Y

Yawping, (probably from yelping) a noisy fellow.
Yit, yet.
Your'n, your own, yours.

Even a casual glance at these words shows that it is misleading to refer to them all as Americanisms. Over 150 of them represent pronunciations more or less common in England and in America before 1815. It is probable that Humphreys' phonetic system, if he had one, is not to be relied on, for he seemed to be able to hear a distinction between such words as *beleve*, *buty*, *jurk*, *shute*, *shure*, *tuff*, and their properly spelled forms. The most interesting-looking pronunciations are indicated by *atarnal*, *briled*, *cuss*, *dasen't*, and *saisse*. *Cuss* is a form attributed to the United States in the *OED*.

The exclamations *swags*, *swamp it*, *vaggers*, *van*, *vumpers*, are interesting and are possibly Americanisms. Dictionary evidence for these forms is scanty.

Ant I is a good expression for people of an ingenious turn of mind to puzzle over. If Humphreys' supposition that it came from "and I" is correct, its use in the passage excerpted is senseless.

Boost, *bread-stuff*, *calculate*, *chirk*, *cleverly*, *quiddles*, *spark*, *stump*, *tarnation*, in the senses indicated by Humphreys, may at present be regarded as Americanisms. They are at least as good candidates for this distinction as can be found in Humphreys' list.

Humphreys thought *darned* could safely be labeled "old English." The makers of the *OED* decided it is chiefly an American expression. Humphreys felt sure *nip* was an Americanism, but the word is found in a 1796 edition of Francis Grose's *Classical Dictionary of the Vulgar Tongue*.

Humphreys' use of the following forms in their indicated meanings is quite early, *awful*, *boost*, *calculate*, *chirk*, *cleverly*, *cuss*, *darned*, *gal*.

Humphreys' Glossary was drawn upon by some of the writers on Americanisms whom we shall have occasion later to mention more fully. Pickering (see p. 65) may not have seen *The Yankey in England* in time to utilize it for his *Vocabulary* published in 1816, but Bartlett (see p. 141) in his *Dictionary of Americanisms* included some words which he got from Humphreys' play. In the *OED* the earliest example of the use of the word *twistical* is taken from *The Yankey in England*.

A great many interesting words and expressions escaped Humphreys when he made up his Glossary. The following expressions and many others of the same nature are to be found in the pages of the play itself:

—send me to look for eggs in a mare's neeste; [p. 21]
I will stur my stumps, and pluck up stakes tu. [p. 32]
—you've got the wrong sow by the ear, [p. 33]
You needn't stick your brussels up so high nuther, to make me sing small. [p. 34]
I am as fine as a fiddle—[p. 37]
I'll be even with you, if it rains pitchforks- [p. 55]
I swouch it. [p. 56]
But these marvellous cummings together, beat old Rose in the gun-room; [p. 87]

The expressions *mare's nest*, *stir one's stumps*, *get the wrong sow by the ear*, *to sing small*, are three or four centuries old at least. *To pull up stakes* is ascribed to the United States in the *OED*, and the earliest citation there given for it is 1830. The expression *to rain pitchforks* occurs in Roget's *Thesaurus* of 1852. *Fine as a fiddle* is not listed in the *OED*, but *fit as a fiddle* is, and the earliest use cited is for 1882.

CHAPTER VI

John Pickering (1777-1846)

SHORTLY after his death John Pickering was referred to as the "most distinguished philologist to which the western continent has given birth." An examination of his life and achievements leaves one with the impression that this praise accorded him was deserved.

His birthplace was Salem, Massachusetts. When he was only a child his father, Timothy Pickering, secretary of state from 1795 to 1800, inspired in him a love for learning that remained with him throughout his life. His opportunities for scholastic attainments were unusual, and he possessed natural endowments that enabled him to make full use of them. Soon after his graduation at Harvard in 1796 he became secretary to William Smith, of South Carolina, United States minister to Portugal.

After spending two years in Lisbon, Pickering was transferred to London as secretary to Rufus King, United States minister at the Court of St. James. Pickering occupied this position two years and then returned to his birthplace and took up the profession of law.

Pickering's zeal for the study of languages began early. He began the study of French at six years of age. He attained such distinction in scholarship, especially along philological lines, that he was offered the professorship of oriental languages at Harvard in

1806, and eight years later the professorship of Greek language and literature. He declined both these offers. He was a competent scholar in English, French, Portuguese, Italian, Spanish, German, Greek, and Latin, and had some acquaintance with Arabic, Turkish, Persian, Sanskrit, and Chinese. There was not anything connected with the study of language that failed to arouse his interest. Possibly his major contribution to scholarship was his Greek-English lexicon which appeared in 1826.

During the two years he spent in London Pickering began the practice of occasionally noting Americanisms and expressions of doubtful authority, "for my own use," as he tells us. This practice on his part resulted finally in his publishing, in June, 1816, the results of his observations with the title *A Vocabulary or Collection of Words and Phrases which have been supposed to be peculiar to the United States of America.* The "Essay" which stands at the beginning of this work is here given.

ESSAY

The preservation of the *English language* in its purity throughout the United States is an object deserving the attention of every American, who is a friend to the literature and science of his country. It is in a particular manner entitled to the consideration of the Academy; for, though subjects, which are usually ranked under the head of *Physical Science*, were doubtless chiefly in view with the founders of the Academy, yet, our *language* also, which is to be the instrument of communicating to the public the speculations and discoveries of our countrymen, seems necessarily "to fall within the design of the institution;" because, unless that language is well settled, and can be read with ease by all to whom it is addressed, our authors will write and publish, certainly under many disadvantages, though perhaps not altogether in vain.

It is true, indeed, that our countrymen may speak and write in a *dialect* of English, which will be understood in the *United States;* but if they are ambitious of having their works read by Englishmen as well as by Americans, they must write in a language that Englishmen can read with pleasure. And if for some time to come it should not be the lot of many Americans to publish works, which will be read out of their own country, yet all, who have the least tincture of learning, will continue to feel an ardent desire to acquaint themselves with *English* authors. Let us then for a moment imagine the time to have arrived, when *Americans* shall no longer be able to understand the works of Milton, Pope, Swift, Addison, and other English authors, justly styled classic, without the aid of a *translation* into a language, that is to be called at some future day the *American* tongue! By such a change, it is true, our loss would not be so great in works purely scientific, as in those which are usually termed works of taste; for the obvious reason, that the design of the former is merely to communicate information, without regard to elegance of language or the force and beauty of the sentiments. But the excellencies of works of taste cannot be felt even in the best translations;—a truth, which, without resorting to the example of the matchless ancients, will be acknowledged by every man, who is acquainted with the admirable works extant in various living languages. Nor is this the only view in which a radical change of language would be an evil. To say nothing of the facilities afforded by a *common language* in the ordinary intercourse of business, it should not be forgotten, that our religion and our laws are studied in the language of the nation, from which we are descended; and, with the loss of the language, we should finally suffer the loss of those peculiar advantages, which we now derive from the investigations of the jurists and divines of that country.

But, it is often asked among us, do not the people of this country now speak and write the English language with purity? A brief consideration of the subject will furnish a satisfactory answer to this question; it will also enable us to correct the erroneous opinions entertained by some Americans on this point, and at the same time to defend our countrymen against the charge made by some English writers, of a *design* to effect an entire change in the language.

As the inquiry before us is a simple question of fact, it is to be determined, like every other question of this nature, by proper evidence. What evidence then have we, that the English language is not spoken and written in America, with the same degree of purity that is to be found in the writers and orators of England?

In the first place, although it is agreed, that there is greater uniformity of dialect throughout the United States (in consequence of the frequent removals of people from one part of our country to another) than is to be found throughout England; yet none of our countrymen, not even those, who are the most zealous in supporting what they imagine to be the honour of the *American* character, will contend, that we have not in some instances departed from the standard of the language. We have formed some *new* words; and to some *old* ones, that are still used in England, we have affixed *new significations:* while others, which have long been *obsolete* in England, are still retained *in common use* with us. If then, in addition to these acknowledgments of our *own countrymen*, we allow any weight to the opinions of *Englishmen*, (who must be competent judges in this case,) it cannot be denied, that we have in several instances deviated from the standard of the language, as *spoken and written in England at the present day*. By this, however, I do not mean, that so great a deviation has taken place, as to have rendered any considerable part of our language unintelligible to Englishmen; but merely, that so many corruptions have crept into *our English*, as to have become the subject of much animadversion and regret with the learned of Great Britain. And as we are hardly aware of the opinion entertained by them of the extent of these corruptions, it may be useful, if it should not be very flattering to our pride, to hear their remarks on this subject in their own words. We shall find that these corruptions are censured, not by mere pretenders to learning, but, (so far as the fact is to be ascertained from English publications,) by all the scholars of that country, who take an interest in American literature. In proof of this, I request the attention of the Academy to the following extracts from several of the British Reviews; some of which are the most distinguished of the present day, and all of which together may be considered as expressing the general opinion of the literary men of Great Britain, who have attended to this subject. That all the remarks are just, to the extent in which they will naturally by understood, few of our countrymen will be willing to admit.*

The *British Critic* (for February 1810) in a review of the Rev. Mr. *Bancroft's* Life of Washington, says—"In the style we "observe, with regret rather than with astonishment, the intro- "duction of several *new* words, or *old* words in a new sense; a "deviation from the rules of the English language, which, if it "continues to be practised by good writers in America, will "introduce confusion into the medium of intercourse, and render "it a subject of regret that the people of that continent should "not have an entirely separate language as well as government "of their own. Instances occur at almost every page; without "pains in selecting, the following may be taken as specimens," &c. The Reviewers then mention several words, all of which are inserted in the following Vocabulary.

The same Reviewers (in April 1808) in their account of Chief Justice *Marshall's* Life of Washington, have the following re- marks:—"In the writings of *Americans* we have *often* discovered "deviations from the purity of the *English idiom*, which we have "been more disposed to censure than to wonder at. The *common* "*speech* of the United States has departed very considerably "from the standard adopted in England, and in this case it is not "to be expected that *writers*, however cautious, will maintain a "strict purity. Mr. Marshall deviates occasionally, but not "grossly," &c.

The *Critical Review* (for September 1809) in remarks upon *Travels through France, by Col. Pinckney*, says—"He falls into "occasional inaccuracies . . . . but the instances are rare, and "by no means so striking as we have *frequent* occasions of remark- "ing in *most American* writers."

The same Reviewers (in July 1807) in speaking of *Marshall's* Life of Washington, have the following among other remarks on the style of that work—that "it abounds with many of those idioms which prevail on the other side of the Atlantic."

* See *Note* at the end of this Essay. [This note is not given in this reprint.—Editor.]

The *Annual Review* (for 1808) in speaking of the same work, after pointing out several instances of false English (in respect to many of which, however, the Reviewers have been misled by the incorrectness of the *English edition* of that work, as will be seen in the following Vocabulary,) has the following observations; which, if they had been made in a manner somewhat different, would probably have been more favourably received by those, for whose benefit they seem to be intended:—"We "have been more particular in noticing these faults in Mr. "Marshall's language, because we are not at all certain that the "Americans do not consider them as beauties; and because we "wish, if possible, to stem *that torrent of barbarous phraseology*, "with which the *American* writers threaten to destroy the purity "of the English language."

The *Monthly Reviewers* (in May 1808) in their account of a little work, entitled *A Political Sketch of America*, cite with approbation, the following passage—"The national *language* should "be sedulously cultivated; and this is to be accomplished by "means of schools. This circumstance demands particular at-"tention, for the language of *conversation* is becoming incorrect; "and even in America *authors* are to be found, who make use of "*new* or *obsolete* words, which no good writer in this country "would employ."

The *Eclectic Review* (for August 1813) in noticing *Sketches of Louisiana, by Major A. Stoddard*, makes the following observations on the style of that author and of our writers in general: "For an American the composition is tolerable; but the Major "has a good share of those words and phrases, which his literary "countrymen must, however reluctantly, relinquish before they "will rank with good writers. The standard is fixed, unless it "were possible to consign to oblivion the assemblage of those "great authors on whose account the Americans themselves are "to feel complacency in their language to the latest ages."

The *Edinburgh Review* (for October 1804) which is the last I shall cite, has the following general observations on this sub-ject:—

"If the men of birth and education in that other England, "which they are building up in the West, will not *diligently study* "the great authors, who purified and fixed the language of our

"common forefathers, we must soon lose the only badge, that
"is still worn, of our consanguinity."

The same Reviewers, in their remarks on *Marshall's* and
Ramsay's Lives of Washington, say—

"In these volumes we have found *a great many words and*
"*phrases* which *English* criticism refuses to acknowledge.
"America has thrown off the yoke of the British nation, but she
"would do well for some time, to take the laws of composition
"from the Addisons, the Swifts and the Robertsons of her
"ancient sovereign. . . . . These remarks, however, are not dic-
"tated by any paltry feelings of jealousy or pride. We glory in
"the diffusion of our language over a new world, where we hope
"it is yet destined to collect new triumphs; and in the brilliant
"perspective of American greatness, *we* see only pleasing images
"of associated prosperity and glory of the land in which we live."

Such is the strong language of British scholars on this subject. And shall we at once, without examination, ascribe it
wholly to prejudice? Should we not by such a hasty decision
expose ourselves to the like imputation? On the contrary, should
not the opinions of such writers stimulate us to inquiry, that we
may ascertain whether their animadversions are well founded or
not? We see the same critics censure the Scotticisms of their
northern brethren, the peculiarities of the *Irish*, and the provincial corruptions of their own *English* writers. We cannot
therefore be so wanting in liberality as to think, that, when
deciding upon the literary claims of *Americans*, they are gov-
erned by prejudice or jealousy. A suspicion of this sort should
be the less readily entertained, as we acknowledge that they
sometimes do justice to our countrymen. The writings of Dr.
Franklin, for example, have received the highest praise; and a
few other American authors have been liberally commended by
them. The opinions of these critics too are supported by those
of some distinguished men in our own country. Dr. *Franklin*
censures, without reserve, "the popular errors several of our
"own states are *continually* falling into," with respect to "expres-
"sions and pronunciation."* Dr. *Witherspoon*, who, by having
been educated in Great Britain, and by his subsequent long

* See the word *Improve* in the following Vocabulary.

residence in the United States, was peculiarly well qualified to judge on this subject, remarks:—"I shall also admit, though with "some hesitation, that gentlemen and scholars in Great Britain "speak as much with the vulgar in common chit chat, as persons "of the same class do in America; but there is a remarkable "difference in their public and solemn discourses. I have heard in "this country in the senate, at the bar, and from the pulpit, and "see daily in dissertations from the press, errors in grammar, im- "proprieties and vulgarisms, which hardly any person of the "same class in point of rank and literature would have fallen into "in Great Britain."*

With these opinions of such distinguished writers before us, shall we entertain the illiberal jealousy that justice is intention- ally withheld from us by our English brethren? Let us rather imitate the example of the learned and modest *Campbell*, who, though he had devoted a great part of a long life to the study of the *English* language, yet thought it no disgrace to make an apology for his *style*, in the following terms: "Sensible," says he, "of the disadvantages, in point of style, which my northern "situation lays me under, I have availed myself of every oppor- "tunity of better information, in regard to all those terms and "phrases in the version, [of the Gospels] of which I was doubt- "ful. I feel myself under particular obligations on this account, "to one gentleman, my valuable friend and colleague, Dr. "Beattie, who, though similarly situated with myself, has with "greater success studied the genius and idiom of our language; "and of whom it is no more than justice to add, that the "acknowledged purity of his own diction, is the least of his "qualifications as an author. But if, notwithstanding all the "care I have taken, I shall be found, in many places, to need the "indulgence of the *English* reader, it will not much surprise me. ". . . . The apology which Irenæus, Bishop of Lyons in Gaul, in "the second century, makes for his language, in a book he pub- "lished in defence of religion, appears to me so candid, so "modest, so sensible, at the same time so apposite to my own "case, that I cannot avoid transcribing and adopting it:—'Non "autem exquires a nobis, qui apud Celtas commoramur, et in

* Druid, No. V.

"barbarum sermonem plerumque avocamur, orationis artem
"quam non didicimus, neque vim conscriptoris quam non
"affectavimus, neque ornamentum verborum, neque suadelam
"quam nescimus.' . . . ."*

Upon an impartial consideration of the subject, therefore, it
seems impossible to resist the conclusion, that, although the
language of the United States has perhaps, changed less than
might have been expected, when we consider how many years
have elapsed since our ancestors brought it from England; yet
it has in so many instances departed from the English standard,
that our scholars should lose no time in endeavouring to restore
it to its purity, and to prevent future corruption.

This, it is obvious, is to be effected, in the first place, by carefully noting every unauthorized word and phrase; or (as Dr.
Franklin many years ago recommended, in his letter to Mr.
Webster on this subject,†) by *"setting a discountenancing mark"*
upon such of them, as are not rendered indispensably necessary
by the peculiar circumstances of our country; and, even if we
should continue to have a partiality for some of those expressions, and should choose to retain them, it will always be useful
to know them. By knowing exactly what peculiar words are in
use with us, we should, among other advantages, have it in our
power to expose the calumnies of some prejudiced and ignorant
writers, who have frequently laid to the charge of our countrymen *in general* the affected words and phrases of a few conceited
individuals;—words and phrases, which are justly the subject
of as much ridicule in *America*, as they are in *Great Britain*. As a
general rule also, we should undoubtedly avoid all those words
which are noticed by English authors of reputation, as expressions with which *they are unacquainted;* for although we might
produce some English authority for such words, yet the very
circumstance of their being thus noticed by well educated
Englishmen, is a proof that they are not in use at this day in England, and, of course, ought not to be used elsewhere by those who
would speak *correct English*.

With a view to this important object I have taken some pains

* Campbell's Four Gospels, preface, p. 28.

† See the word *Improve* in the following *Vocabulary.*

to make a collection of words and phrases, which I offer to the Academy, not as a perfect list of our real or supposed peculiarities of language, but merely as the beginning of a work, which can be completed only by long and accurate observation, especially of intelligent Americans, who shall have an opportunity of residing in England, and of well educated Englishmen who may visit this country. It has long been the wish of our scholars to see a work of this kind; but, though several words have been noticed by Dr. Witherspoon, Dr. Franklin, and some others, yet no one seems to have been willing to undertake the laborious task of making a general collection of them. Seeing no prospect of such a work, and observing, with no small degree of solicitude, the corruptions which are gradually insinuating themselves into our language, I have taken the liberty to ask the attention of the Academy to this subject, by laying before them the following Vocabulary; a performance, which I am sensible is not so worthy of their notice, as it might have been made, had more time and ability been devoted to it.

In making this Vocabulary, I have resorted to all the sources of information in my power, and have, under each word, given some authorities for and against the use of it. I have also subjoined to some of the words, the criticisms of Dr. Franklin, Dr. Witherspoon, and other writers, at large, in order that the reader may avail himself of their instructive observations, without the trouble of searching for them through the numerous volumes of their works; and in all cases, where any word had been noticed by English or American writers, which I had also myself observed, (particularly during my residence in England, where my attention was first directed to this subject,) I have chosen to give it upon their authority, rather than my own. Many words will be found in the collection, which are not in fact of *American origin*, or peculiar to Americans; but it appeared to me that it would be useful to insert all words, the legitimacy of which had been questioned, in order that their claim to a place in the language might be discussed and settled. Several of the words have been obtained from British Reviews of American publications; and I may here remark, how much it is to be regretted, that the reviewers have not pointed out *all* the instances, which have come under their notice, of our deviations from the *English* standard. This would have been doing an essential service to our literature, and have been the most effectual means of accomplishing what those scholars appear to have so much at heart—the preservation of the English language in its purity, wherever it is spoken.

It has been asserted, that we have discovered a much stronger propensity than the English, to add new words to the language; and the little animadversion, which, till within a few years, such new-coined words have met with among us, seems to support that opinion. The passion for these senseless novelties, however, has for some time past been declining. Our greatest danger now is, that we shall continue to use antiquated words, which were brought to this country by our forefathers nearly two centuries ago; (some of which too were at that day *provincial* words in England); and, that we shall affix a *new signification* to words, which are still used in that country solely in their original sense. Words of these descriptions having long formed a part of the language, we are not led to examine critically the authority on which their different significations rest; but those which are *entirely new*, like strangers on their first appearance, immediately attract our attention, and induce us to inquire into their pretensions to the rank they claim.*

But it is not enough for us to note single *words;* our *idiom,* it should seem, is in some degree changed, and is in danger of still greater corruptions.† At the same time, therefore, that we are "setting a discountenancing mark" upon unauthorized words,

---

* The reader will not infer from these remarks, that *our right* to make new words is here meant to be denied. We, as members of that great community or family which speaks the English language, have undoubtedly, as well as the other members, a right to make words and to propose them for adoption into our common language. But unless those, who are the final arbiters in the case, that is, the body of the learned and polite of this whole community, wherever they may be, shall sanction such new terms, it will be presumptuous in the authors of them to attempt to force them into general use. We should hardly be willing to adopt all the words and phrases which the people of Scotland, of Ireland, or of the British Settlements in various parts of the world, should propose to make a part of our common language. Our right however in this respect is not contested by the English themselves: See, for instance, the remark of the *British Critic* on this subject, under the word *Lengthy* in the following Vocabulary.

† That a radical change in the language of a people, so remote from the source of it, as we are from England, is not an imaginary supposition, will be apparent from the alterations which have taken place among the nations of Europe; of which no instance, perhaps, is more striking, than the gradual change and final separation of the languages of Spain and Portugal, notwithstanding the vicinity and frequent intercourse of the people of those two countries.

we should assiduously study the language of the best authors, especially Dryden, Swift, and Addison; to the last of whom, Dr. Blair, in his Lectures on Rhetoric, justly applies Quintilian's well-known remark upon Cicero—that "to be highly pleased "with his manner of writing is the criterion of a good taste in "English style—Ille se profecisse sciat cui Cicero valde place-"bit;" and of whom Dr. Johnson emphatically says—"whoever "would attain a good English style, familiar but not coarse, and "elegant but not ostentatious, must give his days and nights to "the volumes of Addison." Dr. Franklin, who in his *Life* informs us that it was *one of the greatest objects of his ambition to write English well*, formed his style upon that of *Addison;* and Franklin is one of the very few American writers, whose style has satisfied the English critics. This is the discipline to which the most distinguished scholars of Great Britain have submitted, and without which neither they nor the scholars of our own country, can acquire and preserve a pure English style. It is related of Mr. Fox, that when speaking of his intended History, he said, he would *"admit no word into his book for which he had not "the authority of Dryden."** This determination may perhaps seem, at first view, to have been dictated by too fastidious a taste, or an undue partiality for a favourite author; but unquestionably, a rule of this sort, adopted in the course of our education, and extended to a few of the best authors, would be the most effectual method of acquiring a good English style. And surely, if Fox found no necessity for any other words than Dryden had used, those writers have little excuse, who take the liberty, not only of using all the words they can find in the whole body of English authors, ancient and modern, but also of making new terms of their own at pleasure. Who shall have a right to complain of scarcity, where that distinguished orator found abundance? Such standard authors, therefore, should be made the *foundation* of *our English;* but as our language, like all others, is constantly though slowly changing, we should also, in order to perfect our style, as we advance to mature age, study those authors of our own time, who have made the older writers their models. Every word in the writings of Addison, is not now in

* Preface to his *History of James the Second.*

general use, in England; and many words have been adopted since his time, and are now sanctioned by the best writers of that country. These writers, therefore, as well as their illustrious masters, ought to be diligently read; for we should always remember, that in language, as in the fine arts, we can only attain to excellence by an incessant study of the best models.

Pickering's *Vocabulary* deals with slightly more than five hundred words, many of them being words in common use at the present time, and having histories reaching well back into the past. The comments which Pickering makes on the words he selects for special attention are interesting. Under the word *barbecue*, for example, he vindicates "the people of Virginia from the calumnies of prejudiced foreigners" by calling attention to a French translation of a travel-book written by an English visitor to the United States. The French translator wrote, in connection with the word *barbecue:* "Cet amusement barbare consiste à fouëtter les porcs jusqu'à la mort pour en rendre la chair plus delicate. Je ne sache pas que les cannibales mêmes le pratiquent." ("This barbarous amusement is whipping hogs to death in order to make their flesh the more delicate. I do not know that even cannibals practice it.")

Webster wrote Pickering a letter on the subject of the *Vocabulary*, and added a few remarks to those Pickering had made about some of the terms included. The following words appearing in Pickering's list were, so Webster wrote, not familiar to him: *brash* (brittle), *clitchy* (clammy, sticky), *docity* (quick comprehension), *kedge* (brisk), *quackle* (almost to choke), *rafty* (rancid), *slat* (to throw down with violence), *squale* (to throw a rock, stick, etc., so that it skims along the ground), *squat* (to squeeze, mash). Pickering had no doubt heard all these words in New England speech. They also belong to various English dialects and are to be found in Professor Wright's *English Dialect Dictionary*.

Webster concluded his letter to Pickering by offering a suit of clothes—presumably a new suit—to any man "in Great-Britain or America, who will explain our little word *by*, stating its primary signification, and its true sense, in its several uses and applications." Nearly seventy years later Dr. James Murray, editor of the *OED*, first performed the task which Webster outlined. Murray's treatment of *by* occupies about thirteen columns, or more than four large pages, in the *OED*.

CHAPTER VII

Theodoric Romeyn Beck (1791-1855)

THEODORIC ROMEYN BECK was a New York physician and teacher. He was one of the founders of the Albany Institute, an organization having for its object the promotion of science. On March 18, 1829, Dr. Beck read before the Institute an article entitled "Notes on Mr. Pickering's *Vocabulary of Words and Phrases, which have been supposed to be peculiar to the United States.*" This article of Dr. Beck's is here reprinted, being taken from *Transactions of the Albany Institute,* I (1830), 25 ff.

Notes on Mr. Pickering's "Vocabulary of Words and Phrases, which have been supposed to be peculiar to the United States," with preliminary Observations.

By T. ROMEYN BECK.

Read March 18, 1829.

Before a Society composed like the present, it is not necessary to enlarge on the importance of preserving the English Language, whether spoken or written, in its pure state. In what that purity consists, may be the subject of discussion and controversy, but it evidently will resolve itself at last, into that idiom which is in use among the best educated and most enlightened portion of the community. This remark indeed applies to every country, the language of which is not encumbered by dialects. Individuals may be partial to certain words; may deem their omission improper, and may argue that their place cannot be supplied—that no other will convey their precise ideas. But if

78

general custom has dispensed with them, a few voices will not be sufficient to give them currency.

There is however a constant change in all this, agreeing with the mutations to which man and all human works are liable. The popular authors of the last century are no longer the most popular of this: new views are taken of men and things—new modes of expression are invented, and the ever restless and often original mind of man developes untried means by which to convey the ideas which occupy it in such varied profusion. Amidst this alteration, however, there are certain names inscribed on the pages of the history of every nation, to whom all their posterity must do homage and pay deference. The standard writers of a language are, like the guardians of a well ordered state, its preservers from anarchy and revolution. They must be read——and as far as imitation is allowable, must be copied; not with a servile devotion, but a generous emulation. The language they used has been found sufficient to give "a local habitation and a name" to the finest imaginings of poetry and the loftiest flights of oratory. No true admirer would willingly alter it—nor would the idea be tolerated, that it ought to undergo such a change as to render the study of their productions a labour, or even an effort.

Believing then that reason as well as patriotism conspire to teach the importance of a certain degree of stability to a language, it remains to inquire how far innovation, or, if we please, improvement, is proper—Whether the introduction of new words is proper—the revival of obsolete ones, or the remodelling of present ones. With my present object, it is not necessary to go largely into this; but an assertion may be hazarded, that it is apprehended deserves at least some consideration. The warrant to lead in making these changes should be committed to but few. It is not given to many among the host of writers either in this or any other country, fully and completely to understand the multiplied meanings of words; and particularly those which are either foreign or little in use. One of the characteristics of the English Language is its copiousness; and it may be as prudent as it is certainly advisable, first to ascertain the point where its phrases are incapable of expressing the ideas intended to be communicated. Fashion, or the superiority of some great name, sometimes exercises a pernicious influence in this respect. In the days of Dr. Johnson, he sanctioned the introduction of many words from the Latin—In our own time, French words and phrases are thickly strown through the pages of our general literature.

These remarks are only intended as a glance at some of the causes which influence alterations in a language, and as preliminary to a notice of some of the charges which have been made against the citizens of this country, of fostering and increasing innovations in the English Language, as at present in use among the leading writers of Great Britain. By English writers, these are styled *Americanisms*, and they have been noticed with the spirit that characterizes most of the literati of Great Britain when speaking of this country. Overwhelming ridicule and contempt are the elements which form the staple of their criticism, and although in many instances their accusation of coining new words has been found incorrect, by proof that their origin is to be found in some provincial dialect, or some antiquated author, they have seldom had the magnanimity to acknowledge their mistake. This however is merely an objection to the *manner*. The *matter* of their animadversions deserves more serious consideration. Just and necessary, and indeed indispensable, as it is, for us to cultivate all the feelings of an independent nation, yet it behooves us to recollect, that our language is a *derived* one—that our literature is, in one sense, a *foreign* one—and, above all, a living literature, assiduously cultivated in the parent state. The question is, will we conform to it, as it respects language, and thus preserve its harmony and purity, or, allow freedom of innovation. If we permit the last, we shall never arrive at a higher honor than to be placed among those who use dialects. We may, and probably shall, in a few years, present the spectacle of exceeding Great Britain in numbers; but the pride of this annunciation will not be heightened in the mind of any true lover of literature, by the fact, that the most populous nation is introducing words which are unknown to the other.

Views somewhat similar to these have induced several gentlemen in this country to select and notice such words as may be deemed to be improperly used. The utility of this is manifest, as it enables us to view them within a small compass, and properly to impress the necessity of their omission on our minds. Among the best, is to be mentioned the work of Mr. Pickering of Salem, who in his *Vocabulary or Collection of Words and Phrases, which have been supposed to be peculiar to the United States*, at first read before the American Academy of Arts and Sciences, and afterwards published in a separate volume, has made a most valuable collection, and at the same time shown that in many instances, the charges of English writers are either unfair or unfounded. I have endeavored to familiarize myself with its contents, and occasionally have made notes on certain words noticed by him. These are now presented to the Institute.

To Captivate. "To take prisoner—to bring into bondage." This is the definition given by Dr. Johnson, who quotes Shakespeare, King Charles I. and Locke, as authorities. The Edinburgh Review however, in its notice of Bruce's Mineralogical Journal, published in 1810, says—"Other examples, proving the "alteration to which our language has been exposed, chiefly by the "introduction of *Gallicisms*, may be noticed in the rest of the "Journal, resembling expressions found in American newspapers, "where for *a ship taken* we read of *a ship captivated*." Mr. Pickering seems to have been surprised at this charge, but he subsequently found the word in Belknap and Ramsay.*

I may add, that the word is used by Mr. Jefferson in the original draft of the Declaration of Independence. (North American Review, vol. 22, p. 392)—"*captivating and carrying them into slavery.*" It is undoubtedly now an obsolete word in the above sense with English writers, yet I have found it in so modern a one, as Dr. Adam Clarke. In his Reflections on the 42d chapter of Genesis, he says, "The unnatural brethren who sold their brother into captivity are now about to be *captivated* themselves, and the *binder* himself, is bound in his turn."

Citess. This word is noticed by Johnson in the sense of "a city woman," but as peculiar to Dryden. During the stormy period of the French Revolution however, the British Critic, a government Journal, charged the Americans with introducing

* Pickering, p. 55.

this new-fangled word into the English language. They were said to have coined it. The sole authority for this charge is the notorious Peter Porcupine, and he puts the authorship of the term on some violent partisans. All this might have passed in 1796, when men's passions were at the height of irritation, but what shall we think of a literary man, repeating the charge some twenty years or more thereafter? In the review of Inchiquin's Letters in the Quarterly, (vol. 10, p. 500,) it is deliberately stated that the Americans hesitated between *citizeness* and *citess* as the translation of *citoyennes*.

Considerable. Dr. Witherspoon animadverts on the manner on which this is used. *"He is considerable of a Lawyer."* It would seem, however, from the following remark, to have been formerly used in a similar way in England.

Speaking of a story of Ligon in a notice of "Southey's Chronological History of the West Indies," the Quarterly Review, (vol. 38, p. 229,) remarks, *"The story is what our old writers would have called considerable."*

Creek. I mention this word only, to say that we are probably inveterate in diverting it from its old English sense—"a part of the sea which runs into the land."

Thus Milton, (Book 7, line 399,)

> Forthwith the sound and seas, each creek and bay, &c.

We certainly in legislative and other public proceedings, as well as in common language, mean by it a stream smaller than a river. Some of the quotations by Johnson under the word, would seem to permit the present application.

Fall. Autumn. This is certainly not an Americanism, although so charged on us. (Pickering, p. 91.)

Johnson quotes the following lines from Dryden,

> What crowds of patients the town doctor kills,
> Or how *last fall* he raised the weekly bills.

It is remarkable, however, that this is mentioned in one of the earliest accusations brought against this country for coining new words. It is contained in No. 96 of the Mirror, a periodical paper, published at Edinburgh in 1780, and to which Henry Mackenzie, Prof. Richardson, and a number of other Scotch literati, contributed. The article in question was written by Professor Richardson.

"A grave looking man (says he) who sat near me one day at dinner, said a good deal about the *fall* and of events that should have happened before and after the *fall*. As he spoke also about *Providence and Salem and Ebenezer*, and as great deference was shown to every thing he said, and being as I told you, a grave looking man in a black coat, I was not sure but he might be some learned theologian, and imagined he was speaking about Oriental Antiquities and the fall of *Adam*. But I was soon undeceived. The gentleman had lived for some time in Virginia. By Providence he meant the town of that name in Rhode Island, and by the fall he meant not the fall of our first parents, for concerning them he had not the least idea, but as I suppose, the fall of the leaf, for (he adds) the word is used, it seems in the AMERICAN DIALECT for autumn."*

Grade. A friend has pointed out to me the use of this word (in the manner charged by English critics as an Americanism,) in one of the Novels of Sir Walter Scott. It occurs in a dialogue between Lord Menteith and Captain Dalgetty. (Legend of Montrose, Chap. II.) The latter observes, "Why truly, an Irish Cavalier, being major of our regiment, and I having hard words with him the night before, respecting the worth and precedence of our several nations, it pleased him the next day to deliver his orders to me, with the point of his battoon advanced and held aloof, instead of declining and trailing the same, as is the fashion from a courteous commanding officer towards his equal in rank, though it may be his inferior in military GRADE."

To Guess. There is no word, for which New-Englandmen are more teased than this. Almost every English traveller notices it as an Americanism. Yet it is certainly more in the manner, in which it is applied—than because the word is not used. —Mr. Pickering quotes several examples in late works (p. 101.) Even a scholar like Sir Wm. Jones, in an essay before the Society at

---

* Since reading this paper, Mr. M. H. Webster has referred me to Governor Pownall's *Topographical Account of the Middle British Colonies in North America*, London, 1776, in which the word is used. Speaking of the climate in the above portion of country, he says, "Its seasons are "summer, autumn, or what the Americans more expressively call the *fall* and winter," and just below he quotes from Dr. Douglas' history, the following: "At the end of August, as the symptoms of approaching winter begin to appear, we call it the fall of the year." Page 44.

Bengal, when speaking of a doubtful Arabic Couplet, says, "On the whole, I *guess* that the distich should be thus written." *Asiatic Researches*, vol, I, p. 4. I am indebted for this reference to Dr. Coxe. (Emporium of Arts, vol. 1. p. 91.)

Illy. The use of this adverb cannot be too frequently condemned, and it is to be regretted that a man of the eloquence and general accuracy in writing, of Mr. Clay, should have given it the sanction of his example, which he did on taking his seat as Speaker, in December, 1817. I have subsequently seen the word used, in some communication to the Legislature of New-York, but did not the time note, and I cannot now recall it.

Immigration. First used by Dr. Belknap. The Quarterly Reviewers do us the honour of approving its use. They say, (vol. 30, p. 39,) "The Americans have judiciously adopted this word from our old writers. It is one which we should not have suffered to become obsolete."

Locate, as a verb. "This word," says Mr. Pickering, "is not in the English Dictionaries." It is however used. Cumberland in his Memoirs, (p. 318, Amer. Ed.) speaking of Dilly's Entertainments, says, "Here he (Boswell) *has located* some of the liveliest scenes and most brilliant passages in his entertaining anecdotes of his friend Samuel Johnson." And again, in the Edinburgh Review, (vol. 47, p. 88,) speaking of New South Wales, it is remarked, "that the banks of these rivers are fast filling with settlements, those of the Hunter, the nearest to the seat of government, being, we understand, entirely *located*."

In the sense usually applied to the word in this country, it is certainly a technical one, with which we cannot dispense.

Mean used for *Means* by President Munroe in his speech, December, 1817—and criticised by Mr. Coleman. This may rather be called an impropriety than an Americanism. Means is now generally acknowledged as both singular and plural.

Narrate, as a verb. This word has never been directly charged as an Americanism, but has been quoted against us in italics. The Quarterly Reviewers in noticing Dr. McCrie's Life of John Knox, object to his using "the abominable verb *narrate*, which must (say they) absolutely be proscribed in all good writing." It is amusing, in the short space of three years, to find this verb used repeatedly by the same reviewers. In vol. 17, p. 304, speaking of Battel, they say, "*There can be little doubt that he believed what he narrated.*" And again, (vol. 18, p. 539,) "Mr. Sharpe's industry has traced some curious particulars of James Russel, who so coolly *narrates* his own share in this horrible transaction."—*Narrate* is also used by the Rev. Mr. Raffles in his Tour on the Continent. "To explain and *narrate* the story of these unparalleled wonders." (p. 279.) Also in the Foreign Quarterly Review, vol. 1, p. 92.

Nationality. Mr. Pickering says this is used by some writers in America—but although a new word, he has once met with it in the Quarterly Review *in italics.* It is used in the same way in the Edinburgh Review, vol. 6, p. 131. "It is therefore with peculiar regret that we are compelled to advert to the *nationality* of Messieurs Bory & St. Vincent." Dr. Webster also quotes it as used by Boswell.

Respectability. This is a modern word, not to be found in Johnson. It appears to have been used by Cumberland and Kett (*Webster*) and is adopted in the Edinburgh Review, vol. 17, p. 440. It is, however, I apprehend, in more common use in writing in this country than in England.

Sources, as a verb. This is used (certainly improperly) by Mr. Nuttall in his Journey to the Arkansa. (p. 158.) "The main south branch (the Canadian) sources with Red River." Mr. Nuttall is an Englishman by birth, but has been so long resident in this country, that by a species of argument very familiar to reviewers, it may hereafter be called an *Americanism.*

Starvation. This word is neither in Johnson, Webster, or Worcester's Johnson & Walker, and yet it is in general use. I have somewhere seen it mentioned, but cannot state the place, that this word was introduced by Henry Dundas, (afterwards Lord Melville) at the period of the Revolutionary War.

Tarry as a noun. This word is sometimes used in conversation, as "During my tarry in this place," but is not to be found in any dictionary which I have examined. In the London Courier Newspaper of July 7, 1817, it is mentioned that the "Duke of Wellington was on his arrival (at some place) received by a guard of honour, and the band of the 88th continued to play during his Grace's *tarry*, which was merely to take some refreshment."

One who reads Dr. Beck's article is likely to be surprised at finding that such words as *fall*, *grade*, *illy*, *immigration*, etc., have been labeled as Americanisms. Having at our disposal the resources of the *OED*, we are able to find out more about these words than could Dr. Beck and his contemporaries.

Fall, in the sense of autumn, is much more common in the United States than in England, but it did not originate here. *Grade*, in the sense given, is not an Americanism, but when we use the word in such a sentence as "What grade did you make in your history examination?" we employ *grade* in a sense not adequately dealt with in some dictionaries.

Illy is marked dialectal in the *OED*, but excerpts illustrating its use are given from writers such as Jefferson, Southey, Lowell, Irving, and Hardy. There is no evidence that *immigration* experienced a rejuvenation through its early popularity in America. The verb *narrate* came into use later than one might suspect. The earliest citations in which there is no suspicion of the word's being used as a translation of the Spanish *narrar* are as late as the middle of the eighteenth century. Some of the earliest users of *narrate* thought it was of Scotch origin.

Respectability is another word that is comparatively young in our language. The date of the earliest example of its use given in the *OED* is 1785. Evidence of an American origin for the word is lacking.

Starvation is the most interesting word found in Dr. Beck's list. In the first place, it is interesting as being the second oldest noun in English to be made by the affixing of *-ation* to native English verbs. The word having the honor of being the first noun so formed is *flirtation*, dating back to 1718. In the second place, *starvation* possesses interest because it originated in connection with the bill of 1775 "for restraining Trade and Commerce with the New England Colonies." In the debates on this bill there was much said about the undesirability of combating the rebellion by a measure calculated to cause a famine in which the innocent and the guilty would suffer alike. Mr. Dundas, whom Dr. Beck refers to, and who was in favor of the measure, said with reference to the bill that he was afraid it would not produce the famine contemplated. His opponents, among them Walpole and Mason, lost no time in ringing the changes upon this statement, and they used the nicknames "Starvation Dundas" and "Starvation" to refer to its author.

CHAPTER VIII

Mrs. Anne Royall (1769-1854)

WE HAVE so far dealt with New England observations on American English, and we shall next direct attention to observations made in the southern area. It might seem to one not familiar with the facts that southern speech should have been considered before that of New England, since the settlement at Jamestown was earlier than that at Plymouth.

The earliest records kept in the Virginia colony, however, were made either by Englishmen in this country for only a short time or by scribes sufficiently used to the pen to avoid such illuminating deviations from accepted usage as are easily found in the New England records. Consequently, the southern colonial records are not as useful to the student of early American English as are those of the New England colonists.

The earliest commentator on the peculiarities of southern speech whom we shall notice here was Mrs. Anne Royall, a remarkable and somewhat eccentric old lady. Her maiden name was Anne Newport, and she was born in Maryland in 1769. Her girlhood was spent on the frontier where schools were few and far apart. Anne's father, William Newport, was a man of some education and he taught her to read. When she was twenty-eight she married Captain William Royall, a bluff old soldier of the Revolution who had seen hard and honorable service under Lafayette.

After the death of her husband in 1813 and after ten years of litigation over the substantial property which he left behind him, his widow found herself penniless at the age of fifty-four. In her efforts to make a living she became a writer and publisher. She succeeded in making herself one of the most-talked-of women of her day. Although her home was in Washington, D.C., during the last twenty-five years of her life she went all over the United States, soliciting subscriptions for her books and for the newspapers she published. She was a very keen observer, and she commented frequently upon the characteristic features of the speech she heard in the various places she visited. Her comments on the dialect she observed are scattered through her writings in such a way as to make it expedient for us to give here the longer of her comments, indicating after each selection the place from which it is taken.

I

But, to return to my Grison republic;[1] their dialect sets orthography at defiance, and is with difficulty understood; for instance, the words *by*, *my*, *rye*, they pronounce as you would *ay*. Some words they have imported, some they have made out and out, some they have swapped for others, and nearly the whole of the English language is so mangled and mutilated by them, that it is hardly known to be such. When they would say *pretence*, they say *lettinon*, which is a word of very extensive use amongst them. It signifies a jest, and is used to express disapprobation and disguise; "you are just lettinon to rub them spoons—Polly is not mad, she is only lettinon." Blaze they pronounce *bleez*, one they call *waun*, sugar *shugger*; "and is this all it ye got?" handkerchief *hancorchy*, (emphasis on the second syllable;) and "the two ens of it comed loose;" for get out of the way, they

___
[1] This was a community in West Virginia.

say get out of the road: Road is universally used for way; "put
them cheers, (chairs) out of the road." But their favorite word
of all, is *hate*, by which they mean the word thing; for instance,
nothing, "not a hate—not waun hate will ye's do:" What did you
buy at the stores, ladies? "Not a hate—well you hav'nt a hate
here to eat." They have the *hickups*, and corp, (corps,) and are
a *cute* people. Like Shakspear, they make a word when at a
loss: *scawm'd* is one of them, which means spotted. They have
rock houses and rock chimneys, &c. &c.[1]

2

Dialect.—The dialect of Washington, exclusive of the foreigners, is the most correct and pure of any part of the United States
I have ever yet been in. It is very rare that you hear an improper
word, even amongst the common people. A few words are, however, peculiar to them, such as the following, "you're right, he
(or she) did, tantamount to an affirmative." A negative is
signified by "could ever," which means "I will not;" as well as
a general negative. Another phrase is "my dear," used by all
sexes and ages, and upon all occasions: "my dear, when we saw
the cloud, we ran the balance of the way."[2]

3

Respecting the literati of Philadelphia, it is not in my power
to say a word. Nothing would have been more gratifying to me
than to have seen some, at least, of those eminent men, though,
perhaps, I saw the greatest man in the city; I mean Mr. Cary.
From the very limited opportunity I had of judging, I am inclined to think education does not receive that attention we
might expect, in a city so devoted to the public good. The dialect
of the citizens, particularly of the children, gave rise to this opinion; it is very defective, and the young misses are detestably
affected in their manners, dress and dialect. I questioned a few
on the subject of grammar, geography, and history, who were
said to be engaged in these studies, and found them wretchedly

[1] *Sketches of History, Life, and Manners, in the United States* (New Haven,
1826), p. 58.

[2] *Ibid.*, p. 156.

defective. They have, withal, a whining tone in their speech, extremely disgusting; though the higher classes pronounce the English language with purity and even elegance.[1]

4

After limping along about fourteen miles from Nashville, I was compelled to stop, my saddle horse being foundered; and here I am left alone, and *more*—but no matter! All things happen for the best. I will try to beguile the time in amusing myself with "mine host" and hostess, who I dare say, expect to make their Jack out of me—"Old Feginny begging!"* Did you ever see one of your low-bred Virginians—I mean what we call Tuckahoe? The Blue Ridge, you know, as well as I do, separates Virginia into Eastern and Western Virginia, or Tuckahoe and Cohee. Foreigners often distinguish it by the terms Old Virginia and New Virginia. In Old Virginia the lower class of citizens are the most ignorant, presumptuous people in the United States. Well, then, it was one of these bold, arrogant, ignorant, self-important, purse-proud females that constituted the character of my hostess. The old man had not made his appearance, being, as she said, out in the field to look after his hands, (meaning his slaves) for he is rich. My landlady is not homely: she is about forty, low, corpulent, and has a countenance that sets one at defiance. She was all bluster, bustle and anxiety, as if she actually intended to give the lie to the old proverb, that "Rome was not built in a day." She would go out, come in, sit down, get up, and walk to the door and call as loud as if the house were on fire—"Luke, an't you done totin them taters yet?—I 'spose you at the fire again. Sal, you brush them tables off, you hear; take up them ashes, you hear: make up a good fire, you hear† An't Rich'd come with some good water yet? Tha, now, you dun it! What's that? [A servant girl had broken a glass—the landlady runs to see.]—Well, my lady, nev'r mind, I'll pay you fow that—pick um up."

---

* A Virginia phrase.

† I am obliged to retain the *r* in hear, fire, &c. or not be understood; but she *sounded* it not in speaking, nor does any of her sort. *For* they sound like *faw* or *fow*, (light,) and *nor* like *naw*, &c. as "naw you," "naw or na I," &c. and, "what faw," "you hea or he," &c. Also, *tha* for there, and *sharance* for assurance, &c. Nev'r or nev' for never—stars for stairs—mar for mare, &c.

[1] *Ibid.*, p. 229.

In the midst of the scrape a lad came in, who, it seems, was the landlady's son, and had just returned from one of the neighbors. "Well! is it true, that—massy upon me, I bin so hurried I an't had time to pull off my night-cap to-day!—Yond's the old black ho's come up. Sal, go and put him in the stable, and give him some con [corn.] Is it true that Billy's married shoo nuff?" [sure enough.] "Yes!" drones out the boy, no way concerned for his mother's flurries, nor for the passion it was about to throw her into. "Well, now, did ever any body hear the match o' that. Go and tell your daddy to come here. I reckon he'll make him pay the ten dollars he borrowed—he shall smack him with a wan't, [warrant] this very night! Well, it doesn't signify, the sharance some people have. I've wocked [worked] hard for my 'state—but yonders your daddy and Betsy too."

The landlord entered. He was one of your tall, darkskinned, smooth-tongued, sly-looking fellows, that manage matters softly; and quite as low-bred as his spouse. "Fine spot of work! Billy's married, shoo nuff!" Betsy, an awkward lump of mortality, apparently about seventeen, strode across the room to dispose of her bonnet; and finding a stranger in the house, she frisked back, and began to adjust her Feginny cloth dress. Not so, the old lady; but before she opened the flood-gate of her tongue, I made my escape to my chamber. The apartment, however, being on the same floor, I heard the whole lecture distinctly, like a torrent, overwhelming the new married pair. You know how quick those negro-raised Tuckahoes speak: just so did she, never finishing one sentence before she began another.

"Well, it's just as I thought. Wha-t," says the old man? "Oh, it's a fact—John seed'um together." "I wish," replied the wife, "I may never stir, if he oughten to be hanged. I wish I may die!—a good-for-nothing, stinking, lazy—I 'spose you'll lend him ten dollars again. I bound 'twas to pay for his license—well, it don't signify; you will fool away all your 'state—I'd put him in jail, this very night, before he sleeps, that I would. I'll tell him a piece of my mind. Nev'r mind! fa' to have the inshoince to cote [court] my gal! This comes o' larnin gals to write! A darter o' mine shouldn't lan to write, to save her life!—Nev'r mind—

I 'spose he thought I was sich a fool I didn't know what all them letters was about. Tha, now—thar's your thanks faw lett'n him eat here! And so my darter is to be scandalized by sich. . . . ."[1]

5

Bill Cheatum's cleared out. He sarved Tom Marchant the slickest as ever you heard on in all the days o' your life. We was all settin talkin and takin a dram in at Marchant's last Friday, before breakfast, when who should come along, ridin of a critter,* but Bill. I seed he had skins tied behind him; so he hitches his critter, and comes in, and after talkin awhile, and takin a dram, he axed to look at some cloth, and told Marchant to cut off four yards, and takes out a 100 dollar note, and pays for the cloth, and puts the change in his pocket, and axed Marchant if he didn't want to trade for some *coonskins*. Marchant said he didn't care if he did, if they were good. So Bill goes out and brings in the coonskins. Marchant looks at them—very good skins—counted the tails, and axed what for trade he'd make? So, Bill said he'd take same he'd always gave, and would take it in domestic cotton; and the other agreed to it, and the skins lay on the counter. So, after awhile Bill went off, and I went off home, too, and never heard any more of it till yesterday; I was at the store, and Marchant, says to me, says he, "do you think that r—l Cheatum didn't cheat me that day, give me a counterfeit note—and didn't you see how slick he sarved me about the coonskins. Didn't you see the coonskins, and didn't you see the note?" "Yes, says I, I saw the coonskins, and the note, too." "Nothing in the world but possum skins, coontails tied to them, and only bare two coonshins [*sic*] in the whole, one at top and one at bottom." With that he showed me the skins; and sure enough nothing but possum skins, and the note not worth one cent. It's as fair cheatin says I, as ever I seed in my life; and you can make him smoke for it. Yes, says Marchant, but catching's before hanging—the villain's cleared out.[2]

---

* In this country horses are called *critters*—In West Pennsylvania, and West Virginia, they are called beasts.

[1] *Letters from Alabama* (Washington, 1830), pp. 21–23.

[2] *Ibid.*, pp. 103–4.

6

If you wish to ascertain the dialect of a country, you must seek for it amongst the common, or in other words, the lower order of the people, as all well bred people speak alike. But the children of both classes are good specimens of dialect, as the better sort, in this country, particularly, consign their children to the care of negroes. You see I am for another dish of philosophy. But to go on. Those who have black nurses, and those who have illiterate white nurses to attend children, are at much pains and cost for teachers to unlearn them what they need never have learned, had they kept illiterate people from them at first. This is not the case with the poorer class of people, as their children are nursed by themselves, and speak *their* language.

While we were chatting with our neighbor, a number of people rode up to the door, and we went out to see what was the matter. It appeared they were on their return from a barbacue, and had heard a stump speech. Some of these were mere children, and some were grown persons. Our neighbor, who was aware of their business, asked "What news from the barbacue?" "Oh there was a proper sight of people—Oh, my! but there was— You never seed the like! And a heap of 'em had on ruffled shirts, and shoeboots, and was so proud, stepin about; and there was some monstrous purty gals there, and some dinged ugly ones, too; and such a powerful chance of apples and cyder, and ginger cakes. I tell ye what, they were prime; and they made such a fuss, and *covaulted*, and was going to fight; you never saw the like in all the days of your life. Then these fellows that lives on Flint, had like to abin whipped, steppin about. I tell you what, them fellows is monstrous proud; and old F——, was there, too, and got the maddest, he fairly snorted. Oh, he was rearin. And them fellows from Elum's Mill, turned in with old F——, and snorted and covaulted, and dared them ruffle-shirt fellows to turn out. Oh, they got the maddest! And Mr. E—— made a stump speech. He said if we voted for that there 'tother man, I forgot his name, that government would come and take away our land, and we would have to pay taxes and all that." These were mostly Tennesseeans and North Carolinians.

I saw a piece in the papers not long since, which went to

satirize the Tennessee dialect. I would advise such people to look at home. Those who live in glass houses, ought not to throw stones. Let us compare this with the dialect of Virginia. You remember the bear hunting party from Bedford. I will stake them against the whole United States. One of them called at our house on his return, and entertained us with the following account of his adventures: "You know da is heap of baw (bear) on da Kenhawa; so I and Bill Prout, Jess Passin, and Zack Miller, are all goin to Kenhawa to hunt baw—Kenhawa mighty far—so we walk—we walk—last we come to da Kenhawa— Kenhawa b-i-g river, for true—Tell you what, it skears me—well, I goes out into de woods—I hear noise—I look up tree, and see a baw!—I went to da root o' da tree—I bark like any dog— presently da baw come husslin down—Ah, boy!—I took to my keels, and did hook it."—Now for the Pennsylvania dialect: "Jim, where are you and Sam; why but ye's pit (put) you cow in the pester, (pasture;) 'am sure a towled ye's the mornin.— Ye's cruel bad children—and there a fine job ye's done to leave you gears out by." The Yankee: "Flora you want (ought) to wash them clothes right away. You hadn't ought to left 'em so." "What say?"

Covault is of Tennessee birth, and not unaptly applied in the sense they use it. It signifies an unruly or ungovernable man; also an untame horse, or any thing that cannot be controuled. It is quite a classical word, and I hope to see it admitted into the English language. It appears to be a compound of co and vault, which are both very significant. For the rest I find the Tennesseeans are a very plain people, and have a very high sense of honor.[1]

Some of the southernisms which Mrs. Royall called attention to are quite interesting. In selection 1 above we have the odd expression *not a hate*, meaning "not a thing." In the *OED* it is pointed out that this expression is Scottish and originated from *Deil hae't*, "Devil have it." This after becoming a strong negative, equivalent to *Devil a bit*, or "Not a bit," gave

[1] *Ibid.*, pp. 121-22.

rise to the use of haet, hate, in "Not a hate," meaning not a whit or atom.

The form *corp*, selection 1, owes its existence to the feeling on the part of uneducated speakers, that the form *corps(e)*, since it has an *s* sound at the end, is a plural, and should have a singular form without the *s*.

Scawm'd is derived from the verb *scaum*, to scorch or burn. The three expressions just mentioned are Scottish, and they indicate that there were in the "Grison republic" in West Virginia some inhabitants who had Scottish ancestry.

In selection 4 the expression *Old Feginny begging*! and *Feginny cloth* are puzzling. Possibly *Feginny* is a corruption of *Virginia*.

Mrs. Royall's desire expressed in selection 6 that *covault*, our present-day *cavort*, be admitted into the English language has been gratified. The word is now safely housed in the dictionary, but it is still labeled a colloquialism, and does not have much prospect of advancing beyond that status. Mrs. Royall's citation of it as *covault* is the earliest now known.[1]

Scattered through Mrs. Royall's writings there are comments on words and expressions which struck her as being peculiar. In her *Black Book* (Washington, 1828; 3 vols.), I, 148, she explains that a *smoke-house* was "A house where bacon is smoked." Her citation of this expression is the earliest so far found. *Doggery*, *boss*, *evening* (from sundown till bedtime), *stoop* (n.), and *sartin* were among the words she commented upon.

In concluding our examination of Mrs. Royall's observations on dialect we must give in full her ac-

---

[1] The letter in which she used the word was dated April 30, 1821.

count of a bad habit which she thought had an unusual grip upon some of the women in Raleigh, North
Carolina. This account, though full, is appropriate
here, for it gives an excellent explanation of the verb
dip in a sense now happily unknown to most people.
Mrs. Royall's use of the word is the earliest I have
found.

My pen is now to give pain, not only to the parties concerned,
but to all that part of mankind not lost to feeling: I allude to a
strange infatuation of the females in Raleigh, from the oldest to
the youngest, in an unbounded use of snuff!!!—real tobacco
snuff! They do not snuff it up the nose, but take it into the
mouth—they call it dipping. It was first resorted to, to clean
the teeth, and has grown into a confirmed habit! It is simply
dipping a small wooden brush, a little stick (bruised or chewed
at one end) into a common box of snuff and rubbing the teeth,
and they are so besotted, that they sit for hours rubbing their
teeth, merely as it is said, for the pleasure of intoxication—like
a toper over his bottle, which is affirmed to be the effect. But
why snuff would occasion intoxication when grown into a habit,
more than *chewing* tobacco, I cannot discover: some say it is
more apt to reach the system by the saliva. Let this be as it
may, it has a powerful effect on the system, and must finally
destroy the health. The ladies of Raleigh are deadly, pale, and
emaciated, old and young; even little girls look like ghosts. A
knott of young ladies will assemble in a room as though it were
a tea party and lock themselves in, and dip for hours, chatting
and amusing themselves all the while with anecdotes and stories
—cooks, chamber-maids and washer-women, all dip. I have
seen little girls walking in the streets, with their lips besmeared
with snuff and saliva, which rendered them objects of disgust,
and it evidently distends the mouth.

Besides the expense and loss of health, and color, it evidently
must engross all their time. These little and big girls never go
without their box, and the stick in it, either in their reticule or
their bosom; and the cook hardly waits to get her dinner dished,
till she is eagerly engaged in *dipping*. Was there ever such a

thing heard of before! They must be bewitched. Fine women too!—what a pity. It is strange they do not take some measures to stop the evil amongst the children, that the mania might end with the mother. This lamentable practice is said to be spreading into the neighborhood of Raleigh; and, some do say, it is in use in some of the adjoining towns. They generally strive to keep it a secret! but all their vigilance is vain! It is alas! but but [sic] too well known. Several respectable gentlemen, married and single, with deep felt regret, mentioned the ruinous habit to me; and I am sure with the very best intentions, requested me to expose a habit so offensive, and one which threatened to destroy the intercourse of the sexes. The young men of Raleigh, seemed to deplore the unfortunate habit, in language of the most touching sorrow. This is one of the many proofs we have, that women and not men rule the nation. I hope my fair Sisters will never require another public lecture, and that the prospect of dying old maids may induce them to quit *dipping*.[1]

[1] *Mrs. Royall's Southern Tour* (Washington, 1830; 3 vols.), I, 138–39.

CHAPTER IX

Americanisms in the Virginia Literary Museum

IN THE summer of 1829 the *Virginia Literary Museum and Journal of Belles Lettres, Arts, Sciences, &c.*, made its appearance at the University of Virginia. The two men most prominently identified with this new publication were Dr. Robley Dunglison and Professor George Tucker.

Beginning in December, 1829, there was published in the *Museum* a series of articles dealing with Americanisms. Dr. Dunglison is supposed to have written these articles, though they were signed "Wy" in successive issues of the *Museum*. The Americanisms themselves and the prefatory matter preceding the first instalment of them are reprinted here from a copy made for me at the University of Virginia.

AMERICANISMS*

> Words are the people's; yet there is
> a choice of them to be made.
> —BEN JONSON'S *Discoveries*

The observations we have made on the extant English Provincialisms in various numbers of the *Museum* will have already shewn, that many of our reputed Americanisms are common in the Provinces of England. Had Mr. Pickering, indeed, been better acquainted with those dialects he would not have admitted into his diffusive vocabulary many words which find a place there. The number of real Americanisms is small: by which we mean the number of old words used in a new sense; and of *new* words of indigenous origin. Those which were formerly

* From Museum, p. 366.

common in Great Britain and are to be met with in the best writers, which are, in other words, good English, although antient, we would not designate by the term; for, if fashion induces the people of Great Britain to neglect them, we have the right to oppose the fashion and to retain them. They are English words.

The population of our country is of a motley character. In some parts migration has been constantly going on, in others but little change has occurred. The language of the former we should expect to be modified by admixture: the latter should preserve, pretty nearly, its pristine character.

The settlers have been English, Irish, Scotch, French, German, Dutch &c. and wherever the emigrants from any one of these nations have prevailed to a great extent, some of the character impressed by the prevalent population is perceptible. But the English settlers themselves have not all been of the same description: some have proceeded from London and the neighbourhood: others from the west of England and others again from the North: accordingly we find *Cockneyisms*, *west* and *north of Englandisms* in abundance. Many words and expressions, again, are unquestionably of native origin. Some of these are allowable; others ought to be rejected. Those which have been employed to express a state of things not previously existing, which have arisen from the peculiarities of the government or people, belong to the former class; those, which have occurred wantonly and unnecessarily, belong to the latter.

In referring to the words of American growth: under which we have included old words with a new signification and *new* words, we shall adopt the order of Mr. Pickering: omitting, however, those words which he has needlessly canvassed as being incontestibly English, except when a passing remark may be necessary: and adding others, some of them doubtless local, which have escaped him. We regret, in some respects, that we are compelled to undertake this enumeration, without having the Herculean production of Mr. Noah Webster before us, although from what we have seen of it, we should, probably, have been compelled to dissent largely from him, especially in the Etymological department.

The words, not in Pickering, are distinguished by an asterisk.

To *admire*—"to like much, to be very fond of"—In this sense the word is often used in England: as "I admire it much"; but it is not employed as in New England,—in the sentence "I should *admire* to go to Boston."

To *advocate*. "to support." This word, by critics, who were themselves unacquainted with their own language, has been declared an Americanism. İt is no such thing. Milton used it in the same sense. Yet the Encyclopædia Americana seems desirous to claim it, and remarks, that it is doubtful, whether Milton so used it. The author of the article on Americanisms, in that work, cannot have referred to the passage in Milton, or he would have entertained no doubt of the matter:—

"Whether this reflect not with a contumely upon the parliament itself, which thought this petition worthy not only of receiving, but of voting to a commitment after it had been *advocated* and moved for by some honorable and learned gentlemen &c":—*Animadversions* § 1.

Burke also employed it: not at first hand. It came ready made and sanctioned to him.

In Scotland it has a restricted meaning, as in the following sentence.

"For men seldom *advocate* against Satan's works."—*Ruth. Letters*. Here it signifies, "to plead:"—although the Scotch use it in the sense, "to support"—likewise.

Ambition. "spite." a *Virginianism*. "He brought the action against me, for *ambition*."

Applicant—"a diligent student"—not uncommon.

Appreciate, "to rise in value."

Association—"a convention of clergymen"—New England. From this word comes the adjective *associational*.

The tendency to form adjectives from substantives and verbs from substantives is universal.

Letters, in England, are sent by the *post*; and hence "to *post* a letter" has been introduced; or, as we say, by like derivation, "to mail it." To *turnpike* a road is now very common. Originally when tolls were taken, a turnpike was placed upon the footpath; the road subsequently became designated a *turnpike* and afterwards the word was made into a verb. A short time ago, we saw a tavern, recommended in a printed handbill as the most *accommodational* on the road; and in Virginia, we hear of a man intending to "*bacon* his pork."

Backwoodsman. A new term arising out of the circumstances of the country.

Balance. "The remainder of anything"—common over the country. "Won't you spend the *balance* of the evening with me?" In some places, *shank* is quaintly used with the same signification.

*Belting in Virginia—the same as girdling. See "To *girdle.*"

Belittle. Not an Americanism, but an *individualism.*

Bestowment. "The act of conferring"—a barbarism.

*Blizzard. "A violent blow—" perhaps from *Blitz,* [*Germ.*] lightning. *Kentucky.*

*Block. "A row of buildings." "He lives in the same *block* with me." *Common.*

Boatable. "Navigable with boats."—a useful word.

Boating. "Conveying by boats."—not in use in England, but as good a word as *carting* or *ploughing*—we hear also of *wagoning.*

Brash. "Brittle." In this sense the word is American. But it is not difficult to see how it originated. *Brash,* in the North of England, signifies "Twigs or Brush"—slender, fragile branches; and hence it has been used adjectively in the sense of brittle. *New England.*

Bread stuff. "Bread—corn, meal, bread."

To *bridge.* "To make a *bridge*"—an instance of the change alluded to, under *Association. North.*

Brief. Is a *North of Englandism*—as "the wind is brief"—that is, is prevalent or strong. A traveller, hearing the above expression in Virginia, inquired of the driver what the word meant. It meant he replied, "that the wind was a *sort a peart.*"

*Bug. This, in England, is used merely for the bed-bug; except in one or two cases where it has a destinctive [*sic*] epithet —as may-bug, lady-bug, &c. In this country it is applied to almost every insect that flies, but by others is restricted to the Coleoptera.

*Case. Tobacco is said "*to be in case*" when soft and pliant;

or in condition to be packed away in casks without loss. *Southern States*.

*To *catch up*. "To overtake—Kentucky.

Cache. A term used in the western country, for a hole dug in the ground for the purpose of preserving and concealing such provisions and commodities, as it may be inconvenient for the travellers to carry with them. This is from the French, *cacher*, to conceal.

To *calculate*—"to expect"—as "I *calculate* to leave town tomorrow." In Virginia—I *reckon* is used in this sense.

Caucus. "A political, preparatory meeting"—derivation not known. Pickering thinks it is from *Caulker;* these meetings having been first held in a part of Boston, where all the ship-business was carried on.

Cavault or Cavort. Ranting, highflying.—*West*.

Chance. A supply, a quantity—"he lost a right smart *chance* of blood"—vulgarism of the *Southern States*.

Cent. The coin—the *hundredth* part of a dollar.

Centrality. "The quality of being central." *Fr.* a good word.

Checkers or *chequers*. "*Draughts*." The game. A term taken from the chequered state of the board. *New England*.

Church, member of the. "A professor of religion"—both of these phrases are American and technical—"one who has publicly declared his assent to the creed of any church." *Universal*.

Clever. "*Good disposition*." "He is a *clever* fellow but of a week [sic] understanding." The English clever is never applied except to qualities of the head. *New England*.

Clothier. "A fuller or walker." *New England*. In England it is a "seller of cloth."

*To *cohogle*. "To bamboozle." *Kentucky*.

Cob. "The spike of an ear of corn"—a "corn *cob*"—from German *Kopf*—head, and A. Saxon, *cop. Universal*.

To *concur*. "To assent to." "The bill will not be *concurred* by the senate." *Northern States*.

To *conduct*. Used in New England without the pronoun. "He conducts well." Instead of "he conducts himself well."

Congress. Is used by us without the article. English writers generally say "*the Congress*" although they use Parliament without the article. *Congressional* naturally proceeds from the other; and both, arising from the new state of the country, are proper.

Congregational, Congregationalism &c. are technical, and relate to a church government by consent and election.—*Pickering*.

Considerable. As "he is *considerable* of a physician." *New England*.

Connections. "*Relations* by marriage," in contradistinction to those by blood. As "he is a *connection* of mine." *Relations*, in England, includes all.

Consociation and *consociational* are technical—and relate to "a convention of pastors and messengers of churches. *Webster*.

To *Convene.* "To be fit for, or convenient"—as "this road will convene the public, or be convenient for the public." *New England*.

To *cork.* "To shoe a horse with points—or with frost nails." Perhaps from this word, which is old English, comes the *cawker*, quasi *corker*, placed under the wooden shoes of the *Cumbrians*. (See *Dialects of Cumberland*, in *Museum* p. 258.)

Corn. "Indian corn." In England it comprises all the *Cerealia*, used for bread; hence, "*corn* laws"—*corn* market." When applied to the food of the horse in England it means oats singly. *Corn blades*—the leaves of Indian corn. *Southern States*.

Coudeript. Thrown into fits. Kentucky.

County. Mr. Pickering states that this word is sometimes used along with shire; as the county of Hampshire. County and shire mean the same thing. The Pleonasm should be avoided.

Creature. Much employed in New-England for horses, oxen, &c.; this extensive signification is probably obtained from Ireland. In Virginia, the word is often restricted to the horse. "I've got no creature to ride."

Creek. "A small river." *Southern and middle states*.

In New England it has the correct English signification; a part of a sea, lake or river running into the land. Mr. Pickering erroneously limits it to the *sea*.

Dedodgement. "Exit"—Kentucky.

To *depreciate.* "To fall in value;" as "corn *depreciates* fast;" never used as a neuter verb in England.

To *derange.* "To disarrange." We notice this, only to exhibit the absurdity of Pseudo critics. The *British Critic* objected to this word in *Washington's official letters*, after it had actually been used in a previous volume of the very same review. Almost every remark on Americanisms, in that presuming publication, exhibits, that the reviewer was grossly ignorant of his own tongue.

Desk. Sometimes used in New England for the pulpit. In England, there are, in the Episcopalian churches, a reading desk and a pulpit. This may have given rise to the use of the word here.

Dime. From French, *Dime*, the tenth part—a silver coin the value of ten cents.

Disremember. A totally unnecessary word, used in the *Southern states* for "to forget; not remember."

*To district. To lay off into districts.

To *Doom.* "To tax at discretion." *New England.*

Doomage. Is, hence, a fine or penalty.

*Done. A prevalent vulgarism in the *Southern states;* as "*done gone,*" "What have you *done* do?" Only heard amongst the lowest classes; probably obtained from Ireland.

Dutiable. Subject to duties; a very intelligible compound.

Eagle. A gold coin, value ten dollars.

Educational. "Pertaining to education"—like *accommodational,* &c.

*Elegant. This word, like handsome, is employed hyperbolically in the south. We hear of "an *elegant* beef &c."

Equally as. For "equally"—a pleonasm as "equally as well."

*Expect. "Apprehend"—as "I *expect* you left Richmond yesterday."

*Expose. For "exposé"—an exposition. This is very common; and has arisen from the adoption of the word from the French, without accenting the final *e*. (See Museum p. 12.)

Evening. "After dinner." *Southern States.*

Federalist. A new denomination, arising from the political circumstances of the United States.

Fisk or *Fisc.* "The treasury." This is an unpleasant word; although it has been recommended on the high authority of M. Duponceau, and exists in the German and French; both of which had the word from the Latin *fiscus*. It sounds so like fist, as at times, to convey a ludicrous idea to the hearer. "To draw money from the public *fisk*." The word is not needed.

*To *fix*. "To arrange, to prepare." As "I'm *fixing* to go." There is, also, a substantive, "*fix*"—as I'm not in a good *fix*," i.e. I am not prepared. *Southern States*.

Flunkt. "Overcome, outdone." *Kentucky*.

Fodder, in many of the states, means the blades of corn, stacked up for use. In England it is applied to any kind of dry food, stored up for cattle against winter.

To *fort in*. Another case of the substantive being converted into a verb. *Marshall*.

To *fourfold*. "To assess in a fourfold ratio." *Connecticut*. A similar instance.

To *girdle*. "To make a circular incision through the bark of trees and leave them to die." (*See Belting*.)

Givy. "Muggy." The weather is said to be givy, when there is much moisture in the atmosphere. *South*.

Good. "*Well*." A vulgarism in the southern states. As "I can't fix it *good*."

Gouging. This word has been borrowed from the carpenters [*sic*] shop. It is taken from the old English word, employed by old Ben. "To *gouge*," i.e. to scoup out as with a gouge or chisel.

——— by googing of 'em out
Just to the size of my bottles, and not slicing.
    —*Devil is an Ass*

Grade. "Degree, order." This word is now in common use. We see no objection to it. It has honorable ancestry both in the Teutonic and Romanic stocks.

Happifying. "Making Happy." A barbarous term of hybrid origin—half Latin and half English. It is occasionally heard from the pulpit.

Handsome. Is more extensively used in this country than in England. There they would rarely or never speak of a "*handsome* garden;" although the term is now more extensively applied there than formerly.

Heap. Much—a great quantity or number. *Southern and Western States*. As "it is a *heap* colder to day." A *heap* of pains, a *heap* of dollars. It corresponds with the word *lots* as it was commonly used in England, some years ago.

Help. "A servant." *New England.* Generally a "female servant."

Hominy or *hommony.* "Food made of Indian corn, broken coarsely and bruised." *General.*

*Honeyfuggle. "To quiz, to cozen." *Kentucky.*

*Hoppergrass. This word is often used in the south for *grasshopper. A vulgarism.*

*Hornswoggle. "To embarrass irretrievably." *Kentucky.*

Illy. This adverb cannot, perhaps, be said to be of American origin; it has, however, been employed by so few of the older English writers; and is now never used in England, that we mention it here. *Ill* is equally an adverb and adjective; and hence, *illy*, to say the least of it, is unnecessary.

To *improve.* "To occupy, make use of, employ"—as to "*improve* as a tavern"—"to *improve* a schoolmaster." "to *improve* their children in labour &c." *New England.*

Improvement, of a sermon, the conclusion. *New England.*

In for *into*, and *vice versa.* This is said to be common in New York and Pennsylvania. "We get *in* the stage," and have the rheumatism *into* our knees. *Coleman* "When did you come *in* town." *Pennsylvania.*

Insularity. "The situation or state of an island." A convenient word, and one that has been coined from the Latin, in England as well as this country.

Interval-land or *Interval.* "Bottomland." *New England.*

Involvement for "involvedness." Used by Mr. Marshall in his *Life of Washington.*

*Join the church—"to become a "member of the church." See *church member of the.*

To *keep.* "To stay at the house of any person." "Where do you *keep?*" *New England.*

Lecture day. "A holiday"—from the custom of excusing boys from going to school on those *week* days, when there was a public lecture.

Lay. "Terms or conditions of a bargain, prices, wages;"—as "I bought the articles at a good *lay.*"

Lengthy. "Long, lengthened, extended, prolix."

Lick, or *salt lick.* "A salt spring; the earth which has been furrowed by the deer and buffalo licking the earth on account of the saline particles with which it is impregnated."

Like, for "*as* or *like as.*" "He carries them *like* I do"—a vulgarism in the *southern* and *western states;* it is also used, as follows, in the south: "I do not feel *like* eating." *Vulgarism.*

Likely. "Sensible, intelligent, of moral worth." *New England.* The word is, also, frequently employed in the sense of "*good looking;*" as "he is a *likely* fellow." Mr. Pickering quotes a sentence from the *Portfolio,* in which it is asserted, that the word, in the latter sense, is used throughout the British dominions. We believe it to be very rarely so employed, in any part of England. It seems to be obsolete. In Scotland it is used.

> Off *likely* men that born was in Ingland.
> Be suerd and fyr that nycht deit v thousand.
> —*Wallace* M.S.

Lister from *List.* One who receives and makes returns of ratable estate." *Connecticut.*

To *locate.* "To place, to reside"—"a number of courts properly *located.*" "Where do you intend *to locate?*" Or "where are you *located?*" The word is used also in the sense of, "to designate a tract by writing or to fix the boundaries of unsettled land." *Webster.*

Location. "The act of designating and bounding land;" also "the tract so designated."

Lot. "A field or part of premises." As "keep your cow out of my *lot.*"

*To *lot* or *allot,* (with upon) "to court [*sic*] upon"—as, "I *lot* upon going thither." *New England.*

Lumberer. "A seller of timber." *North.*

**Marooning.* Perhaps from *mare* the sea. It always means a "*party to the sea shore.*" *South Carolina.* Also common in the West Indies.

**Means.* Medicine. *South.*

**Measurably.* In a measure.

Merchant. This word, in England, is applied to a person engaged in traffic with foreign countries. In many parts of the United States, it means a retail dealer, also.

To *missionate.* "To perform the functions of a missionary," It is characterized in Pickering's *Vocabulary* as a low, unauthorized word.

Moccason or *Moggason.* According to Webster, "a shoe of soft *lether** without a sole, ornamented round the ankle." *Indian.*

*Mosey. "To move off. *Kentucky.*

*Motivity. "The quality of being influenced by motives;" also "the power of producing motion." *Dwight.*

*Mollagausauger. "A stout fellow." *Kentucky.*

Mush. "Food of cornmeal, boiled." *Southern States.*

Musical. "Humorous"—as "he is very *musical." Local,* in *New England.*

Netop. An Indian word for "a friend or crony." *Massachusetts.*

*Nitre. This word is very improperly used, in many parts, for "the *sweet spirit of nitre,*" instead of for salt-petre.

To *notify.* "To inform." This is an American signification; and, hence, "to *notify* him of it," is common. The real interpretation of the word is "to make known;" and the sentence ought to be "to notify it to him." This error is universal. (See *Museum* p. 12.)

Notions. "Small wares." As "Yankee *notions." New England, Vulgarism.*

Offset. Not uncommonly employed for "*set off.*"

On. As "*on* tomorrow;" a mere expletive. *Common.*

Organize. To "arrange." This word has a restricted sense, being applied to political and other bodies; as, "have you *organized?*;" i.e. have you arranged?

Over for *under.* "A writer *over* the signature." This ridiculous and unjustifiable innovation has been already criticized in this Journal. (p. 12.)

To *packet.* "To ply with a packet." This is a local word; originating from the substantive, like many others; as to *cart,* to *wagon,* &c.

Pappoose. The Indian name for "a child"; applied to Indian children.

To *Parade.* "To assemble, arrange, exhibit, bring forth." "Come, *parade* your jewels."

---

* Amongst the many idle innovations introduced by Webster in the established orthography of the language, this is one. Why did he not begin at home and strike out the expletive, *h,* from his own christian name?

Pine-barren. "A forest of pines." *Carolinas.*

*Plunder. "Luggage, effects." A vulgarism in the *Southern States.* As "your *plunder* (effects) has arrived."

Portage. "A carrying place, by the banks of rivers, round waterfalls or rapids." *North.*

Prairie. "A natural meadow, or a plain naturally destititute [*sic*] of trees." A word introduced from the French.

Prayerful—prayerfully, used by some of the clergy—but not English.

To *predicate.* "To found," as "my proposition was *predicated* on that view." Very commonly used.

Professor of Religion. See *Member* of the church. We there stated that these words are American. We might have said Scotch likewise.

To *Progress.* "To advance." The verb "to prog'ress" [*sic*] is used by Shakspeare.

Proxies. "Written votes or ballots."

Rhode Island and Connecticut. Also, "the election or election-day." *Prox* is, also, used in Rhode Island for "the ticket or list of candidates at elections."

Publishment of the banns—for "publication." *New England. Local.*

*To quiddle. "To busy one's self about trifles." The word is also used as a substantive. *New England.*

*To quit. "to leave off"—as "*quit* it, I say!" *Southern States.*

Rackets. "Snow shoes." *New England.*

To *raise.* "To bring up, to cultivate"—as "to *raise* corn." "I was *raised* in Virginia."

Redemptioner. "One who redeems himself by services or whose services are sold to pay certain expences."

*To reflunk. "To retreat, to back out." *Western States.*

Renewedly. "Anew, again."

Result. A technical name for "the decision of ecclesiastical councils." *New England.*

To *result.* "To decide or decree as an ecclesiastical council." "The council *resulted* that the parties &c.

*Retiracy. "Solitude." *Western States.*

Rock for "stone." He heaved a *rock.*" "He threw a stone"—a refinement.

Rowdy. "A low, dirty fellow—a blackguard." *West*.

Rooster. "A cock"—a refinement. *Local*.

Rugged. "Robust"—as "a *rugged* child." *New England*.

Run. "A small stream. *Common*.

Samp. "Corn broken coarsely, boiled and mixed with milk." Indian.

Sauce. "Every common, esculent vegetable." *New England*.

Sauce marketers. "Farmers who supply the markets with vegetables. *New England*.

Scow. "A large, flat bottomed boat," perhaps from the Hollandish, *Schuyt*.

Season. Weather—as "a good *season* for planting." *South*.

Section. "Part, quarter" &c. as "in this *section* of the country."

Sectional. From section—"local"—as "*sectional*, feelings;" i.e. local feelings.

Shote. "A young hog." this [*sic*] is often considered an Americanism. It is common in the south east of England and was used generally in Minsheu's time,—"*Shots* porcos dicunt qui unicum agunt annum."

Slang whanger. "A noisy talker or newspaper writer."

Sled. "A carriage for heavy articles on the snow." *New England*.

Sleigh. "A snow carriage for the conveyance of light articles." *New England*.

Sniptious and Ripsniptious. "Smart, spruce." *South and West*.

Sockdologer. "A decisive blow"—one, in the slang language "Capable of setting a man a thinking."

Sparse. "Thin, settled here and there. *Universal*.

Span. Perhaps from the German *Gespann*—"a pair"—as "a *span* of horses." New England.

Spell. "A fit, a period," as a *spell* of sickness. *General*.

Spile. "A spigot."

Splendid. This word is used more hyperbolically than in England—as "a *splendid* piece of beef."

Springy. "Active, agile." *New England*.

Squatter. "A person who enters upon new lands and cultivates them without permission of the owners."

To *squiggle*. "To move about like an eel." *New England vulgarism.*

Staging. "Scaffolding"—*General.*

Stalled. A wagon set fast in the road is said to be *stalled.*

Store. "A shop"—this is not used in England: although it is in some of the colonies.

Suability. "liability to be sued."

Stud. "A stallion:" "to take the *stud*"—to be obstinate: originally applied to a horse that refuses to go on.

Subscriber. "The undersigned:" as "the subscriber informs his friends" &c. (See *Museum* p. 3.)

Succotash. "A mixture of new, soft maize and beans boiled." *Indian.*

To *Systemize.* "To reduce to a system."

Tartar. "Tartar Emetic"—an unwarrantable use of the word: *Tartar* means crystals of Tartar—cream of Tartar. The misnomer might be the cause of accidents.

To *Tote.* "To carry, convey, remove, to carry on the back."— This word is common in Massachusetts and in the southern states. If we mistake not, Mr. Webster considers it a word introduced by the negroes. This is improbable. To *Tolle* from Lat. *Tollere* is an old word, signifying to take away, and Tolt is an old law term, thus defined by Minsheu. "*Tolt*, tolta, is a writ whereby a cause depending in a court Baron is removed into the county court." We are probably, therefore, indebted to the law for it.

Town. "A district of certain limits; also, the inhabitants or legal voters of a town"—*Webster.—New England.*

Trade. "Doctor's trade:" that is "drugs or medicine." The same as *truck. New England.*

Truck. See *Trade.*

Ugly. "Ill tempered, bad," as "he is an *ugly* fellow." i.e. of a bad disposition, wicked. *New England.*

To *Variate.* A word used by the clergy, as "*variate* of thy mercies according to our circumstances." It is not English.

Vine. "Any creeping plant." In England it is restricted to the plant that bears the grape.

*To *Whip*. "To beat,"—as "my dog can *whip* yours." *Vulgarism. Southern States.*

CHAPTER X

Western and Southern Vernacular

WE HAVE seen that the peculiar character of southern speech elicited many comments and much condemnation from Mrs. Anne Royall. Some of Mrs. Royall's observations (see pp. 88 ff.) indicate that she had encountered in her southern travels a type of speech which was more or less definitely associated with the area usually referred to in the early part of the nineteenth century as the West. This West embraced, roughly speaking, the area south of the Ohio River and west of the Allegheny Mountains. It will be interesting to notice somewhat carefully the kind of speech that was regarded as typical of this region during the second quarter of the past century.

At that time the "land beyond the mountains" had not lost in popular imagination a certain glamor of romantic mysteriousness which from an early time was associated with "the dark and bloody hunting ground." To people dwelling in the comparatively effete East, western Kentucky and Tennessee was a faraway region, inhabited by painted savages and ferocious animals, among whom dwelt pioneer Indian fighters and keelboatmen like David Crockett, Ben Hardin, and Mike Fink who carried on the traditional heroism brought over from the days of Daniel Boone and the other "long hunters."

Men such as these were in the popular fancy of the

time invested with a kind of picturesqueness that, after a fashion, still clings about their names. When Andrew Jackson, whom the "yaller flowers of the forest," these "half-horse half-alligator" men of the West, claimed as one of their own, was elected president of the United States the westerners of that day came into political and literary prominence.

When David Crockett went to Washington in 1827, having been elected to Congress from a district in Tennessee, he found that people came long distances to stare at him, "the man from the cane," as they termed him. He was regarded as a kind of embodiment of the West that was thought to be sparsely inhabited by two-fisted fighters, gougers, and unerring riflemen. Interest was so keen in the western type of character that much fiction depicting western life and exploits was produced by such writers as James K. Paulding, R. M. Bird, Judge A. B. Longstreet, and others.

The thing that makes this western type of frontiersman interesting in this connection is that there was used—or thought to be used—by these westerners a vernacular that was regarded as characteristic of them and of their region. The following list of words with their meanings indicates fairly accurately the language level of the more colorful portion of the borderers' vocabulary:

Absquatulate, v. to go away

Blizzard, n. a violent blow
Blustiferous, a. blustery, violent
Bodyaciously, adv. wholly, completely
Breadbasket, n. stomach

Capersome, a. lively
Cavort, v. to rear, plunge, frisk

Circumsurround, v. to surround completely
Clamjamphrie, n. trumpery, rubbish
Clodpolish, a. awkward, like a rustic
Cohogle, v. to confuse, confound, overcome
Conbobberation, n. a commotion, confusion
Cornucked, p.p. thrown into fits

Creature comfort, n. whiskey

Dadshamed, p.p. confounded, "cussed"
Darnation, n. damnation
Dashy trashy, a. trifling, worthless
Dedodgment, n. exit

Exflunctify, v. to wear out, "use up"
Explaterate, v. to explain, talk
Explicitrize, v. to censure

Flagratious, a. flagrant
Flambergast, v. flabbergast, astonish
Flipperty-gibbet, adv. at once
Flugens, interj. used to indicate strong
    feeling
Flummuck, v. to outdo, overcome

Gemornetty, interj. used to express sur-
    prise
Giraffed, p. p. humbugged
Grandiferous, a. extremely well

Helliferocious, a extremely ferocious
Honeyfuggle, v. to cheat
Hornswoggle, v. to embarrass

Johnny cake, n. a kind of bread

Killniferously, adv. fondly

Lickspittle, n. a bootlicker, contempti-
    ble person
Locumsgilly, v. to overcome

Mollagausauger, n. a bully, stout fellow

Monstracious, a. huge, monstrous
Monstropolous, a. monstrous

Obflisticate, v. to do away with
Odoriferous, a. excited, wrought up
Over-scrumptious, a. overparticular

Peedoddles, n. some sort of nervous dis-
    order
Pestiferous, a. pesky
Puckerstopple, v. to embarrass

Rampoose, v. to go on a rampage
Rapscallionly, adv. rascally
Ripsniptiously, adv. in a fiery, lively
    manner
Rumbunctious, a. hot-tempered

Sevagerous, a. very savage
Sharp-set, a. hungry
Shy, n. trial, chance
Singecate, n. violent-tempered person
Sizzled, p.p. drunk
Skirmudgeon, n. rascal
Slang-whanger, n. an orator
Slooney, n. a nincompoop
Snow-storm, n. a kind of drink
Sockdologer, n. heavy blow
Sumtotalize, v. to sum up
Suspicion, n. a very small amount
Swipey, a. drunk

Tetotaciously, adv. completely

Wrap-rascal, n. hunting shirt

In addition to a large number of words like these
there was attributed to the "yaller flowers" a long
list of expressions such as *one of the blue hen's chickens,
to kick the bucket, burnt brandy won't save him, to see
how the cat jumps, a huckleberry over my persimmon,
knock into a cocked hat, too high for picking cotton* (i.e.
drunk), *to pick a crow with one, to cut one's eyeteeth, to
go the whole hog, to root hog or die, knee high to a frog,
slick as goose grease,* etc.

It would of course be a mistake to suppose that this

western vocabulary was altogether concocted by the borderers. Some of the expressions attributed to the "Valley Kings," and "River Rollers," might have been coined by them, but a large part of their vernacular speech was made up of words that had been in existence a long time but had either grown obsolete or had never occupied a place of honor or respectability in the language.

Writers who tried to depict western character in the eighteen-thirties and eighteen-forties made generous use of words and phrases like the foregoing. One of the popular plays of the day was *The Raw Kentuckian, or the Lion of the West*, written by James K. Paulding, and featuring Nimrod Wildfire, who, many people thought, was drawn from life, David Crockett being the model. This play is no longer in existence, so far as I know, but there are newspaper accounts of it, and the following extract from the play itself, apparently, is given here from the *Daily Louisville Public Advertiser* for October 17, 1831.

The *Lion of the West*, was played on Friday evening, and drew a crowded house, notwithstanding the inclemency of the weather. The principal character in this production, is, to use his own elegant language, a *screamer*. Some idea of his peculiarities may be formed from the following slight sketch which he gives of an affair between himself and a raftsman.

'I was ridin' along the Mississippi in my wagon, when I come acrost a feller floatin' down stream, settin' in the starn of his boat fast asleep! Well, I had'nt had a fight for ten days—*felt as tho' I should have to kiver myself up in a salt barrel to keep'*—so Wolfy about the head and shoulders. So, says I, "hulloa, strannger! if you dont take keer your boat will run away with you!" So he looked up at me slantindicler, and I looked down on him slantindiclar—he took out a chor o' tobaccer, and says he, 'I dont value you tantamount to *that!*" and then the varmint flapped his wings and crowed like a cock. I ris up, shook my mane, crooked my neck, and neighed like a horse. He run his boat plump, head-foremost ashore. I stopped my wagon and sot my triggers. "Mister," says he, "I can whip my weight in wild-cats, and ride straight through a crab-apple orchard on a flash of lightning. Clear meat-ax disposition; the best man, if I a'nt, I wish I may be tetotaciously exfluncted!"

The two belligerents join issue, and the Colonel goes on to say—

'He was a pretty severe colt, but no part of a priming to such a feller as me. *I put it to him mighty droll*—in ten minutes he yelled Enough! and swore I was a rip-staver! Says I, *"A'nt I the yaller flower of the forest!* and I'm all brimstone but the head, and that's aquafortis!" Says he, *"Stranger, you're a beauty!* and if I only know'd your name, I'd vote for you next election. Says I, "my name is Nimrod Wildfire—half horse, half alligator and a touch of the airthquake—that's got the prettiest sister, fastest horse and ugliest dog in the District, and can outrun, outjump, throw down, drag out and whip any man in all Kaintuck.'

From this short account of the play we can easily understand why one English visitor who saw it given in Philadelphia was unable to understand it; to him it was a jumble of unintelligible idioms.

This "highfaluting," "helliferocious" sort of expression has, in the main, disappeared along with the people who were supposed to use it. As a passing speech type it differed sharply from the southern provincial speech of the time, to which we shall now give some attention.

The longest list of southern provincialisms that I know anything about is that prepared by Rev. Adiel Sherwood (1791–1879), who was born in New York and educated in New England. Because of his poor health he moved to Georgia, and in 1827 published the first edition of his *Gazetteer of the State of Georgia*. In this work Sherwood included a short list of provincial expressions. Two years later in a second edition he left out the provincialisms, but in a third edition of 1837 he included on pages 69 ff. a much fuller list which, with its introductory paragraph, is given below.

PROVINCIALISMS

The following List is not inserted, because we are the only people who coin and use words without regard to accuracy; but with the hope that seeing them printed, we shall forbear to drag them into service. It will be seen by reference that many of our Provincialisms are borrowed from England. There is no section of country, but has more or less of them.

Arter, for after.
Ager, for ague.
Arrant, for errand.
Ary, for either.
Aint, for is not, and am not.
Axd, for asked.
Aig, for egg.
Abul, for able.
Appeereunce, for appearance.
Alabam, for Alabama.
Assign, for sign; *assign* is to convey away property; *sign* is merely to write the name.

Blotch, for blot—a stain or spot. There is the word blotch; but it signifies a pustule, or spot on the skin.
Blather, for bladder.
Brickly, for brittle.
Beneth, for beneath.
Bess, for best.
Bar, for bear, a beast.
Bresh, for brush.
Becase, for because.
Breethering, for brethren.
Bornd, for born; this is sometimes written so in the lists of births in Bibles.
Board, for a horse for feeding or keeping.

Bodaciously, wholly.
Beyant, for beyond.
Babtises, for Baptists.
Beast, or *crittur*, for horse.

Choosed, for chose.
Crap it, for crop it.
Cotch'd, for caught.
Com'd, for came.
Chunck, for chump.
Cheer, for chair.
Chimbly, for chimney.
Crap, for crop.
Christiun, christian.
Capting, for captain.
Charrackter, character.
Convenunt, convenient.
Crossway, causeway.
Charot, chariot.
Carry a horse to water, instead of lead or ride him to water.
Crazy, for sickly or weakly.

Dare, for there.
Dairter, for daughter.
Disremember, for misremember.
Drownded, for drowned.
Digging, dear or costly—*i.e.* a mighty *digging* price.
Derange, disarrange.

Difficulted, perplexed.
Don did it, for has done it.
Done said, for has said.
Determd, determined.
Discurse, for discuss.
Do dont, do not.
Drap, for drop.
Done said it, for has said it.
Done did it, for has performed, or done it.

Et, for ate.
Erro, error.
Expeerunce, experience.
Eend, for end.

Fare, for far.
Flustrate, frustrate.
Feller, for fellow.
Fermiliar, familiar.
Fout, for fought.
Flitters, for fritters.
Forks of Road, fork.
Febuary, February.
Frozed and *freezed*, for frozen.
Fight, for chastise; equals *fight*, but a master *chastises* his servant.
Fix, for fit or prepare. To *fix* is to fasten: to *fit* is to make ready, &c.
Fix, for situation or condition—*bad fix.*
Fauch, for fetch, or bring.

Gim me, for give me.
Guardeen, guardian.
Guzzle, for gurgle.
Garding, garden.
Gal, for girl.
Great big, large.
—This word is used variously—*great* christian, for pious man; *great* horse is applied to a small poney—meaning a horse of good qualities and bottom; *great* plantation, a fertile one.
Grievyous, grievous.
Gone with, become of—what is *gone with it* or with him, for become of it or him.
Go by, for call, or stop at.
Get shet of, for get rid of.
Hit, for it.

Haint, for have not.
Hadn't ought, for ought not.
His'n, for his.
Handkercher, handkerchief.
Howsomever, however.
Hope, help.
—The obsolete verb *holp* was in use 200 years ago.
Harricane, hurricane.
Hime, for Hymn.
Holt, for hold.
Hath, for hearth.
Helt, for held.
Handwrite, handwriting.
Heap, for much or many: A *heap* of birds flying, or deer running, seems odd. *Heap* of speeches: as the words drop from the speaker, seems also improper. A *heap*, of logs or bushes is correct.
Heavun, for heaven.
Hyether, for hither.
Hender, for hinder.
Hurted, for hurt.
Hen-aig, for hen's egg.
Holpe, for help.

Intrust, for interest.
Ingon, for onion.
Illdisposed, for indisposed.
Ignomeenious, for ignominious.
Imposture, for impostor.
I is and you is, for I am and you are.
Illconvenient, inconvenient.
Impotent, for important.
Inimy, for enemy,

Jemes, James.
Jest for just.
Jine, for join.
Jesu's love, Jesus' love. We do not say Mose's, nor should we say Jesu's.

Knowed, for knew.
Kiver, for cover.
Keerless, for careless.
Kaintuc, for Kentucky.

Like I do, for as I do; *like* can never be used before a nominative: *like me* or *him* is proper.
Loss, for lose; he *loss* it, for loses it or lost it.

Learn, for teach; I will *learn you* is incorrect; the pupil *learns*—the teacher *teaches* his pupil, but does not *learn* him.
Lather, for ladder.
Lay, for lie; do you *lay* down to rest, for do you *lie down*.

Mighty big, for very big; mighty is an adjective, and so is big—but the design of the speaker is not to use two adjectives, but to express some quality in regard to the adjective with an adverb; *very* is an adverb, and expresses some circumstance in regard to big.
Mounting, for mountain.
Mountaneous, for mountanious.
Met up with, for overtook.
Mout, might.
Marchant, for merchant.
Massissippi, for Mississippi.
Mushmillion, for Muskmelon.
Maracle and *muracle*, for miracle.
Monstrous, for very, as monstrous great.
Mighty, for very, as mighty well, &c.
May be he cant, for an affirmation that one can do, or perform a thing.
Misery, for pain, as misery in my head.
Mout, for might.
Marci, for Mercy.

Norard, northward.
Nary one, neither.

Overseed, for took oversight.
Oxens, oxen.
Obsarver, for observer.
Obedunce, obedience.
Overplush, overplus.
One'st, for once.
Opinuated, conceited.

Pillow, for pillar.
Pillar, for pillow.
Pervision, provision.
Paculiar, peculiar.
Perserves, for preserves.
Prasbattery, for Presbytery.
Perdigious, for prodigious.
Primary, for predicament.

Perpeetual, for perpetual.
Prevade, for pervade.
Pertition, petition.
Power, for much or many, *i.e.* he has read *a power*—he has a *power* of corn or negroes—he can lift a *power*.
Pardner, for partner. If it *was please* God, for if it please God.
Pree, for prey, (pr'pray) spoil.
Plunder, for goods, effects or booty.
Proud, for glad, as I should be proud to see you.
Pleasantry, for pleasure.
Pertend up, for better, more cheerful.

Queshton, for question.

Ramsack, for ransack.
Rench, for rinse.
Rech, for reach.
Resk, for risk.
Rock, for stone;—he threw a *rock* at me; *stone* is the proper word, There are rocks, stones, and pebbles: the first are large and unmanagable by the hand; the second, the stones, are smaller and can be thrown. David slung a *stone* at Goliath; but it would have required Sampson to have cast a *rock*.
Reverent, for strong;—*reverent whisky*,. *i.e.* not diluted.
Raised, for brought up;—for I was *raised* in such a county, should be brought up or educated. We raise horses, cattle and swine; but not human beings.
Right good, for very good.
Rared, for reared;—he was *rared*, or he *rared*; *Reared* is the proper word—to educate, or elevate, is the meaning.
Ruff, for roof.

Scoripin, scorpion.
Skeersely, scarcely.
Streetch, for stretch.
Speret, for spirit.
Seed, saw.
Set, sit.

Set, sat;—hen's *set:* You *set* an arm, a post, or a chair; but he *sits* to-day or sat yesterday.
Squinch, for quench.
Scace, for scarce.
Slim, for small.
Stars, for stairs.
Sarment, for sermon.
Scrouge, for crowd.
Squash, for quash.
Saft, for soft.
Sacer, for saucer.
Stairs, for stars.
Sartin, for certain.
Strot for strut.
Sparrow-Grass, for asparagus.
Scriptorean, scripturist.
Smart chance, for good deal, large quantity, large company, great number.
Severals, for several.

Teached, for taught.
Tuther, other.
Tower, for tour—(pronounced *toor*)
Tater, for potatoe.
Tollible, tolerable;—*sorter tollible*, for tolerably well.
This year, or *this 'ere*, for this.
Two times, twice.
Two foot, two feet.
Two mile, for two miles.
Tuck, for took.
Thurst, for thrust;—he *thurst* his hand into his bosom.
Terro, for terror.
Tight scrouging, for difficult.
Twell, for till;—twell night—twell next week.
Twis't, for twice.
Them are, for those.
Tex and *texes*, for text and texts.
Tremendeous, for tremendous.
Tribunial, for tribunal.
This 20 years, for these 20 years.

Tote, for carry or bear; this is from the Latin *tollit*—he carries. It became *tolt* in English—and then as *holpe* fell to hope, so has *tolt* to tote. *Tolt* is frequently found in old English books.
This long, or *that long*, for so long.
This far, for so far.
Truck, for medicine.
Truck, for produce, cloth, or almost any thing.

Unly, for only.
Um, for them.
Umberillo, for umbrella.
Ultimate, for terminate.
Used, for feed;—the sheep *used* in that field.
Use-to-could, for could formerly;—I *used-to-could* do it.

Varment, for vermin.
Villion, villain.

Water-million, for water-mellon.
Wary, weary. *Wensday*, Wednesday.
Weeky-day, week day.
While, for till; *i.e.* stay *while* I come, for stay *till* I come.
Went, for have gone;—you ought not to have *went* is improper; it should be have *gone*.
Wur, for were.
Whole heap, for many, several, much, large congregation.
Wrench, for rinse.

Yaller, for yellow.
Yearly, for early;—come right *yearly*, &c., for come soon or early.
Yont, for yonder; —as *yont* house.
Yearb, for herb.
Year, for here;—come right *year*, for come here.

Without going elaborately into an examination of these expressions we may label the following as Americanisms: *fix, nary, plunder, reverent, rock, smart chance, tote, truck.*

It is somewhat remarkable that Sherwood, a minister, did not recognize in *carry a horse to water* an excellent example of "carry" used as it is in the Bible. In II Kings 9:2 the King James Version has:

> And when thou comest thither, look out there Jehu the son of Jehoshaphat the son of Nimshi, and go in, and make him arise up from among his brethren, and carry him to an inner chamber.

CHAPTER XI

James Fenimore Cooper (1789-1851)

JAMES FENIMORE COOPER is too well known to require any introduction. The following essay of his is taken from *The American Democrat, or Hints on the social and civic relations of the United States of America* (Cooperstown, 1838), pages 117–24.

ON LANGUAGE

Language being the medium of thought, its use enters into our most familiar practices. A just, clear and simple expression of our ideas is a necessary accomplishment for all who aspire to be classed with gentlemen and ladies. It renders all more respectable, besides making intercourse more intelligible, safer and more agreeable.

The common faults of American language are an ambition of effect, a want of simplicity, and a turgid abuse of terms. To these may be added ambiguity of expression. Many perversions of significations also exist, and a formality of speech, which, while it renders conversation ungraceful, and destroys its playfulness, seriously weakens the power of the language, by applying to ordinary ideas, words that are suited only to themes of gravity and dignity.

While it is true that the great body of the American people use their language more correctly than the mass of any other considerable nation, it is equally true that a smaller proportion than common attain to elegance in this accomplishment, especially in speech. Contrary to the general law in such matters, the women of the country have a less agreeable utterance than the men, a defect that great care should be taken to remedy, as the nursery is the birth-place of so many of our habits.

The limits of this work will not permit an enumeration of the popular abuses of significations, but a few shall be mentioned, in order that the student may possess a general clue to the faults. "Creek," a word that signifies an *inlet* of the sea, or of a lake, is misapplied to running streams, and frequently to the *outlets* of lakes. A "square," is called a "park;" "lakes," are often called "ponds;" and "arms of the sea," are sometimes termed "rivers."

In pronunciation, the faults are still more numerous, partaking decidedly of provincialisms. The letter *u*, sounded like double *o*, or *oo*, or like *i*, as in vir*too*, for*tin*, for*tinate*; and *ew*, pronounced also like *oo*, are common errors. This is an exceedingly vicious pronunciation, rendering the language mean and vulgar. "New," pronounced as "*noo*," is an example, and "few," as "*foo*;" the true sounds are "*nu*" and "*fu*," the *u* retaining its proper soft sound, and not that of "*oo*."

The attempt to reduce the pronunciation of the English language to a common rule, produces much confusion, and taking the usages of polite life as the standard, many uncouth innovations. All know the pronunciation of p l o u g h; but it will scarcely do to take this sound as the only power of the same combination of final letters, for we should be compelled to call t h o u g h, thou; t h r o u g h, throu; and t o u g h, tou.

False accentuation is a common American fault. Ensign (insin,) is called en*syne*, and engine (injin,) en*gyne*. Indeed, it is a common fault of narrow associations, to suppose that words are to be pronounced as they are spelled.

Many words are in a state of mutation, the pronunciation being unsettled even in the best society, a result that must often arise where language is as variable and undetermined as the English. To this class belong "clerk," "cucumber" and "gold," which are often pronounced as spelt, though it were better and more in conformity with polite usage to say "clark," "*cow*cumber," (not cow*cum*ber,) and "goold." For *looten*ant (lieutenant) there is not sufficient authority, the true pronunciation being "*levten*ant." By making a familiar compound of this word, we see the uselessness of attempting to reduce the language to any other laws than those of the usages of polite life, for they who affect to say *looten*ant, do not say "*looten*ant-co-lo-nel," but "*looten*ant-kurnel."

The polite pronunciation of "either" and "neither," is "i-ther" and "ni-ther," and not "eether" and "neether." This is a case in which the better usage of the language has respected derivations, for "*ei*," in German are pronounced as in "height" and "sleight," "*ie*" making the sound of "*ee*." We see the arbitrary usages of the English, however, by comparing these legitimate sounds with those of the words "lieutenant colonel," which are derived from the French, in which language the latter word is called "*co-lo-nel*."

Some changes of the language are to be regretted, as they lead to false inferences, and society is always a loser by mistaking names for things. Life is a fact, and it is seldom any good arises from a misapprehension of the real circumstances under which we exist. The word "gentleman" has a positive and limited signification. It means one elevated above the mass of society by his birth, manners, attainments, character and social condition. As no civilized society can exist without these social differences, nothing is gained by denying the use of the term. If blackguards were to be *called* "gentlemen," and "gentlemen," "blackguards," the difference between them would be as obvious as it is to-day.

The word "gentleman," is derived from the French gentilhomme, which originally signified one of noble birth. This was at a time when the characteristics of the condition were never found beyond a caste. As society advanced, ordinary men attained the qualifications of nobility, without that of birth, and the meaning of the word was extended. It is now possible to be a gentleman without birth, though, even in America, where such distinctions are purely conditional, they who have birth, except in extraordinary instances, are classed with gentlemen. To call a laborer, one who has neither education, manners, accomplishments, tastes, associations, nor any one of the ordinary requisites, a gentleman, is just as absurd as to call one who is thus qualified, a fellow. The word must have some especial signification, or it would be synonymous with man. One may have gentleman-like feelings, principles and appearance, without possessing the liberal attainments that distinguish the gentleman. Least of all does money alone make a gentleman, though, as it becomes a means of obtaining the other requisites, it is usual to give it a place in the claims of the class. Men may be, and often are, very rich, without having the smallest title to be deemed gentlemen. A man may be a distinguished gentleman, and not possess as much money as his own footman.

This word, however, is sometimes used instead of the old terms, "sirs," "my masters," &c. &c., as in addressing bodies of men. Thus we say "gentlemen," in addressing a publick meeting, in complaisance, and as, by possibility, some gentlemen may be present. This is a license that may be tolerated, though he who should insist that all present were, as individuals, gentlemen, would hardly escape ridicule.

What has just been said of the word gentleman, is equally true with that of lady. The standard of these two classes, rises as society becomes more civilized and refined; the man who might pass for a gentleman in one nation, or community, not being able to maintain the same position in another.

The inefficiency of the effort to subvert things by names, is shown in the fact that, in all civilized communities, there is a class of men, who silently and quietly recognize each other, as gentlemen; who associate together freely and without reserve, and who admit each other's claims without scruple or distrust. This class may be limited by prejudice and arbitrary enactments, as in Europe, or it may have no other rules than those of taste, sentiment and the silent laws of usage, as in America.

The same observations may be made in relation to the words master and servant. He who employs laborers, with the right to command, is a master, and he who lets himself to work, with an obligation to obey, a servant. Thus there are house, or domestic servants, farm servants, shop servants, and various other servants; the term master being in all these cases the correlative.

In consequence of the domestic servants of America having once been negro-slaves, a prejudice has arisen among the laboring classes of the whites, who not only dislike the term servant, but have also rejected that of master. So far has this prejudice gone, that in lieu of the latter, they have resorted to the use of the word *boss*, which has precisely the same meaning in Dutch!

How far a subterfuge of this nature is worthy of a manly and common sense people, will admit of question.

A similar objection may be made to the use of the word "help," which is not only an innovation on a just and established term, but which does not properly convey the meaning intended. They who aid their masters in the toil may be deemed "helps," but they who perform all the labor do not assist, or help to do the thing, but they do it themselves. A man does not usually hire his cook to *help* him cook his dinner, but to cook it herself. Nothing is therefore gained, while something is lost in simplicity and clearness by the substitution of new and imperfect terms, for the long established words of the language. In all cases in which the people of America have retained the *things* of their ancestors, they should not be ashamed to keep the *names*.

The love of turgid expressions is gaining ground, and ought to be corrected. One of the most certain evidences of a man of high breeding, is his simplicity of speech; a simplicity that is equally removed from vulgarity and exaggeration. He calls a spade, a "spade." His enunciation, while clear, deliberate and dignified, is totally without strut, showing his familiarity with the world, and, in some degree, reflecting the qualities of his mind, which is polished without being addicted to sentimentalism, or any other bloated feeling. He never calls his wife, "his lady," but "his wife," and he is not afraid of lessening the dignity of the human race, by styling the most elevated and refined of his fellow creatures, "men and women." He does not say, in speaking of a dance, that "the attire of the ladies was exceedingly elegant and peculiarly becoming at the late assembly," but that "the women were well dressed at the last ball;" nor is he apt to remark, "that the Rev. Mr. G—— gave us an elegant and searching discourse the past sabbath," but, that "the parson preached a good sermon last sunday."

The utterance of a gentleman ought to be deliberate and clear, without being measured. All idea of effort should be banished, though nothing lost for want of distinctness. His emphasis ought to be almost imperceptible; never halting, or abrupt; and least of all, so placed as to give an idea of his own sense of cleverness; but regulated by those slight intonations that give point to wit, and force to reason. His language should rise with the subject, and, as he must be an educated and accomplished man, he cannot but know that the highest quality of eloquence, and all sublimity, is in the thought, rather than in the words, though there must be an adaptation of the one to the other.

This is still more true of women than of men, since the former are the natural agents in maintaining the refinement of a people.

All cannot reach the highest standard in such matters, for it depends on early habit, and particularly on early associations. The children of gentlemen are as readily distinguished from other children by these peculiarities, as by the greater delicacy of their minds, and higher tact in breeding. But we are not to abandon all improvement, because perfection is reached but by few. Simplicity should be the first aim, after one is removed from vulgarity, and let the finer shades of accomplishment be acquired as they can be attained. In no case, however, can one who aims at turgid language, exaggerated sentiment, or pedantic utterance, lay claim to be either a man or a woman of the world.

Cooper's comments on *ensyne, engyne,* and *cowcumber* show that he was in favor of having the stress come early in these words. On *ensign* and *engine* the stress is now uniformly placed on the first element. The form *cowcumber* is not used much nowadays to refer to a cucumber.

The pronunciation of *lieutenant* which Cooper indorsed is now rarely if ever heard in America, and our pronunciation, *lootenant,* as he represented it, is practically unknown in England. For some reason that cannot be made out the pronunciation which Cooper indicated by *levtenant* has won general approval in England. Dr. Henry Bradley, who edited the word for the *OED,* was not able to account for the present English pronunciation or for the corresponding forms, *lieftenant, levtennant, leftenant,* etc. It is a good word to bear in mind and twit our English friends with when they are disposed to find fault with our reckless use of the language. *Lieutenant* comes straight from French and should have in English the pronunciation which Cooper objected to. Cooper's point about the inconsistency involved in pronouncing the first word in *lieutenant colonel* somewhat after the French fashion—that is, *lootenant*—and anglicizing the second word *colonel* into *kurnel* is well taken, but in the realm of language we are accustomed to inconsistency.

The pronunciation *goold,* to rhyme with *cooled,* though it found favor with Cooper, has now so completely disappeared that one may be surprised to learn that it was a very common pronunciation during the early nineteenth century.

Help, in the sense Cooper mentioned, is an Americanism and may still be heard in colloquial use.

CHAPTER XII

English Travelers

PEOPLE from England who visit this country sometimes comment on the language they hear in the United States. Frequently these British friends of ours deplore the fate that has befallen the King's English in this country.

These comments by our English brethren never do any harm to anyone, and we should feel glad at all times to have them. In these later and more degenerate days, however, the comments and criticisms have paled out considerably. They no longer make us angry as they used to, and for that reason maybe, as well as for others, they are not made as frequently as they formerly were.

The golden age for English travelers who commented on our abuse of language was the first half of the nineteenth century. Hundreds of travelers from England visited the United States then, and in a surprisingly large number of cases they wrote books about their experiences here. Not infrequently in their books these travelers gave long comments on the language used in the new nation.

From a great number of these observations which might be given I have selected the following because it comes from the pen of Captain Frederick Marryat, the celebrated novelist and naval officer who visited America in 1837–38 and published at Philadelphia in 1839 his *Diary in America with remarks on its institutions*. Our selection is from II, 30–40.

LANGUAGE

The Americans boldly assert that they speak better English than we do, and I was rather surprised not to find a statistical table to that effect in Mr. Carey's publication. What I believe the Americans would imply by the above assertion is, that you may travel through all the United States and find less difficulty in understanding, or in being understood, than in some of the counties of England, such as Cornwall, Devonshire, Lancashire, and Suffolk. So far they are correct; but it is remarkable how very debased the language has become in a short period in America. There are few provincial dialects in England much less intelligible than the following. A Yankee girl, who wished to hire herself out, was asked if she had any followers, or sweethearts? After a little hesitation, she replied, "Well, now, can't exactly say; I bees a sorter courted, and a sorter not; reckon more a sorter yes than a sorter no." In many points the Americans have to a certain degree obtained that equality which they profess; and, as respects their language, it certainly is the case. If their lower classes are more intelligible than ours, it is equally true that the higher classes do not speak the language so purely or so classically as it is spoken among the well-educated English. The peculiar dialect of the English counties is kept up because we are a settled country; the people who are born in a county live in it, and die in it, transmitting their scites of labour or of amusement to their descendants, generation after generation, without change: consequently, the provincialisms of the language become equally hereditary. Now, in America, they have a dictionary containing many thousands of words which, with us, are either obsolete, or are provincialisms, or are words necessarily invented by the Americans. When the people of England emigrated to the States, they came from every county in England, and each county brought its provincialisms with it. These were admitted into the general stock; and were since all collected and bound up by one Mr. Webster. With the exception of a few words coined for local uses (such as *snags* and *sawyers*, on the Mississippi,) I do not recollect a word which I have not traced to be either a provincialism of some English county, or else to be obsolete English. There are a few from the Dutch, such as *stoup*, for the porch of a door, &c. I was once talking with an American about Webster's dictionary, and he observed, "Well now, sir, I understand it's the only one used in the Court of St. James, by the king, queen, and princesses, and that by royal order.'

The upper classes of the Americans do not, however, speak or pronounce English according to our standard; they appear to have no exact rule to guide them, probably from a want of any intimate knowledge of Greek or Latin. You seldom hear a derivation from the Greek pronounced correctly, the accent being generally laid upon the wrong syllable. In fact, every one appears to be independent, and pronounces just as he pleases.

But it is not for me to decide the very momentous question, as to which nation speaks the best English. The Americans generally improve upon the inventions of others; probably they may have improved upon our language.

I recollect some one observing how very superior the German language was to the English, from their possessing so many compound substantives and adjectives, whereupon his friend replied, that it was just as easy for us to possess them in England if we pleased, and gave us as an example an observation made by his old dame at Eton, who declared that young Paulet was, without any exception, the most *good-for-nothingest*, the most *provoking-people-est*, and the most *poke-about-every-cornerest* boy she had ever had charge of in her life.

Assuming this principle of improvement to be correct, it must be acknowledged that the Americans have added considerably to our dictionary; but, as I have before observed, this being a point of too much delicacy for me to decide upon, I shall just submit to the reader the occasional variations, or improvements, as they may be, which met my ears during my residence in America, as also the idiomatic peculiarities, and having so done, I must leave him to decide for himself.

I recollect once talking with one of the first men in America, who was narrating to me the advantages which might have accrued to him if he had followed up a certain speculation, when he said, "Sir, if I had done so, I should not only have *doubled* and *trebled*, but I should have *fourbled* and *fivebled* my money."

One of the members of Congress once said, "What the honourable gentleman has just asserted I consider as *catamount* to a denial;"—(catamount is the term given to a panther or lynx.)

"I presume," replied his opponent, "that the honourable gentleman means *tantamount*."

"No, sir, I do not mean *tantamount;* I am not so ignorant of our language, not to be aware that *cat*amount and *tan*tamount are *an*onymous."

The Americans dwell upon their words when they speak—a custom arising, I presume, from their cautious, calculating habits; and they have always more or less of a nasal twang. I once said to a lady, "Why do you drawl out your words in that way?"

"Well," replied she, "I'd drawl all the way from Maine to Georgia, rather than *clip* my words as you English people do."

Many English words are used in a very different sense from that which we attach to them; for instance: a *clever* person in America means an amiable good-tempered person, and the Americans make the distinction by saying, I mean English clever.

Our *clever* is represented by the word *smart*.

The verb *to admire* is also used in the East, instead of the verb *to like*.

"Have you ever been at Paris?"

"No; but I should *admire* to go."

A Yankee description of a clever woman:—

"Well, now, she'll walk right into you, and talk to you like a book;" or, as I have heard them say, "she'll talk you out of sight."

The word ugly is used for cross, ill-tempered. "I did feel so *ugly* when he said that."

Bad is used in an odd sense: it is employed for awkward, uncomfortable, sorry:—

"I did feel so *bad* when I read that"—awkward.

"I have felt quite *bad* about it ever since"—uncomfortable.

"She was so *bad*, I thought she would cry," sorry.

And as bad is tantamount to *not good*, I have heard a lady say, "I don't feel *at all good*, this morning."

Mean is occasionally used for ashamed.

"I never felt so mean in my life."

"We reckon this very handsome scenery, sir," said an American to me, pointing to the landscape.

"I consider him very truthful," is another expression.

"He stimulates too much."

"He dissipates awfully."

And they are very fond of using the noun as a verb, as—

"I *suspicion* that's a fact."

"I *opinion* quite the contrary."

The word *considerable* is in considerable demand in the United States. In a work in which the letters of the party had been given to the public as specimens of good style and polite literature, it is used as follows:—

"My dear sister, I have taken up the pen early this morning, as I intend to write *considerable.*"*

The word great is oddly used for fine, splendid.

"She's the *greatest* gal in the whole Union."

But there is one word which we must surrender up to the Americans as their *very own*, as the children say. I will quote a passage from one of their papers:—

"The editor of the *Philadelphia Gazette* is wrong in calling absquatiated a Kentucky *phrase* (he may well say phrase instead of *word*.) It may prevail there, but its origin was in South Carolina, where it was a few years since regularly derived from the Latin, as we can prove from undoubted authority. By the way, there is a little *corruption* in the word as the *Gazette* uses it, *absquatalized* is the true reading."

Certainly a word worth quarrelling about!

"Are you cold, miss?" said I to a young lady, who pulled the shawl closer over her shoulders.

"*Some*," was the reply.

The English *what?* implying that you did not hear what was said to you, is changed in America to the word *how?*

"I reckon," "I calculate," "I guess," are all used as the common English phrase, "I suppose." Each term is said to be peculiar to different states, but I found them used every where, one as often as the other. *I opine*, is not so common.

---

* Life and Remains of Charles Pond.

A specimen of Yankee dialect and conversation:—

"Well now, I'll tell you—you know Marble Head?"

"Guess I do."

"Well, then, you know Sally Hackett."

"No, indeed."

"Not know Sally Hackett? Why she lives at Marble Head."

"Guess I don't."

"You don't mean to say that?"

"Yes, indeed."

"And you really don't know Sally Hackett?"

"No, indeed."

"I guess you've heard talk of her?"

"No, indeed."

"Well, that's considerable odd. Now, I'll tell you—Ephrim Bagg, he that has the farm three miles from Marble Head— just as—but now, are you sure you don't know Sally Hackett?"

"No, indeed."

"Well, he's a pretty substantial man, and no mistake. He has got a heart as big as an ox, and every thing else in proportion, I've a notion. He loves Sal, the worst kind; and if she gets up there, she'll think she has got to Palestine (Paradise;) arn't she a screamer? I were thinking of Sal mysel, for I feel lonesome, and when I am thrown into my store promiscuous alone, I can tell you I have the blues, the worst kind, no mistake—I can tell you that. I always feel a kind o' queer when I sees Sal, but when I meet any of the other gals I am as calm and cool as the milky way," &c. &c.

The verb "to fix" is universal. It means to do any thing.

"Shall I *fix* your coat or your breakfast first?" That is— "Shall I brush your coat, or *get ready* your breakfast first?"

Right away, for immediately or at once, is very general.

"Shall I fix it right away—*i.e.* "Shall I do it immediately?"

In the West, when you stop at an inn, they say—

"What will you have? Brown meal and common doings, or white wheat and chicken *fixings;*"—that is, "Will you have pork and brown bread, or white bread and fried chicken?"

Also, "Will you have a *feed* or a *check?*"—A dinner, or a luncheon?

In *full blast*—something in the extreme.

"When she came to meeting, with her yellow hat and feathers, was'n't she in *full blast?*"

But for more specimens of genuine Yankee, I must refer the reader to Sam Slick and Major Downing, and shall now proceed to some farther peculiarities.

There are two syllables—*um, hu*—which are very generally used by the Americans as a sort of reply, intimating that they are attentive, and that the party may proceed with his narrative; but, by inflection and intonation, these two syllables are made to express dissent or assent, surprise, disdain, and (like Lord Burleigh's nod in the play) a great deal more. The reason why these two syllables have been selected is, that they can be pronounced without the trouble of opening your mouth, and you may be in a state of listlessness and repose whilst others talk. I myself found them very convenient at times, and gradually got into the habit of using them.

The Americans are very local in their phrases, and borrow their similes very much from the nature of their occupations and pursuits. If you ask a Virginian or Kentuckian where he was born, he will invariably tell you that he was *raised* in such a county—the term applied to horses, and, in breeding States, to men also.

When a man is tipsy (spirits being made from grain,) they generally say he is *corned*.

In the West, where steam-navigation is so abundant, when they ask you to drink they say, "Stranger, will you take in wood?"—the vessels taking in wood as fuel to keep the steam up, and the person taking in spirits to keep *his* steam up.

The roads in the country being cut through woods, and the stumps of the trees left standing, the carriages are often brought up by them. Hence the expression of, "Well, I am *stumped this time.*"

I heard a young man, a farmer in Vermont, say, when talking about another having gained the heart of a pretty girl, "Well, how he contrived to *fork* into her young affections, I can't tell; but I've a mind *to put my whole team on*, and see if I can't run him off the road."

The old phrase of "straining at a gnat, and swallowing a

camel," in the Eastern States, rendered "straining at a *gate*, and swallowing a *saw-mill*."

To *strike* means to attack. "The Indians have struck on the frontier;"—"A rattle-snake *struck* at me."

To make tracks—to walk away. "Well, now, I shall make tracks:"—from foot-tracks in the snow.

Clear out, quit, and put—all mean "be off." "Captain, now, you *hush* or *put*"—that is, "Either hold your tongue, or be off." Also, "Will you shut, mister?"—*i.e.* will you shut your mouth? *i.e.* hold your tongue?

"Curl up"—to be angry—from the panther and other animals when angry raising their hair. "Rise my dander up," from the human hair; and a nasty idea. "Wrathy" is another common expression. Also, "Savage as a meat-axe."

Here are two real American words;—

"Sloping"—for slinking away;

"Splunging," like a porpoise.

The word "enthusiasm," in the south, is changed to "entuzzy-muzzy."

In the Western States, where the raccoon is plentiful, they use the abbreviation *'coon* when speaking of people. When at New York, I went into a hair-dresser's shop to have my hair cut; there were two young men from the west—one under the barber's hands, the other standing by him.

"I say," said the one who was having his hair cut, "I hear Captain M—— is in this country."

"Yes," replied the other, "so they say; I should like to see the *'coon*."

"I'm a *gone 'coon*" implies "I am distressed—*or* ruined—*or* lost." I once asked the origin of this expression, and was very gravely told as follows:—

"There is a Captain Martin Scott* in the United States army who is a remarkable shot with a rifle. He was raised, I believe, in Vermont. His fame was so considerable through the State, that even the animals were aware of it. He went out one morning with his rifle, and spying a raccoon upon the upper branches of a high tree, brought his gun up to his shoulder; when

---

* Already mentioned in the Diary.

the raccoon, perceiving it, raised his paw up for a parley. "I beg your pardon, mister," said the raccoon, very politely; "but may I ask you if your name is *Scott?*"—"Yes," replied the captain.—"*Martin* Scott?" continued the raccoon.—"Yes," replied the captain.—"*Captain* Martin Scott?" still continued the animal.—"Yes," replied the captain, "Captain Martin Scott?" —"Oh! then," says the animal, "I may just as well come down, for I'm a *gone 'coon*." "

But one of the strangest perversions of the meaning of a word which I ever heard of is in Kentucky, where sometimes the word *nasty* is used for *nice*. For instance; at a rustic dance in that State, a Kentuckian said to an acquaintance of mine, in reply to his asking the name of a very fine girl, "That's my sister, stranger; and I flatter myself that she shews the *nastiest* ankle in all Kentuck."—*Unde derivatur*, from the constant rifle-practice in that State, a good shot, or a pretty shot, is termed also a nasty shot, because it would make a *nasty* wound: *ergo*, a nice or pretty ankle becomes a *nasty* one.

The term for all baggage, especially in the south or west, is "plunder." This has been derived from the buccaneers, who for so long a time infested the bayores and creeks near the mouth of the Mississippi, and whose luggage was probably very correctly so designated.

I must not omit a specimen of American criticism.

"Well, Abel, whot d'ye think of our native genus [*sic*], Mister Forrest?"

"Well, I don't go much to theatricals, that's a fact; but I do think *he piled the agony up a little too high* in that last scene."

The gamblers on the Mississippi use a very refined phrase for "cheating"—"playing the advantages over him."

But, as may be supposed, the principal terms used are those which are borrowed from trade and commerce.

The rest, or remainder, is usually termed the balance.

"Put some of those apples into a dish, and the *balance* into the store-room."

When a person has made a mistake, or is out in his calculation, they say, "You missed a figure that time."

In a skirmish last war, the fire from the British was very

severe, and the men in the American ranks were falling fast, when one of the soldiers stepped up to the commanding officer and said, "Colonel, don't you think that we might compromise this affair?" "Well, I reckon I should have no objection to *submit it to arbitration* myself," replied the colonel.

Even the thieves must be commercial in their ideas. One rogue meeting another, asked him what he had done that morning; "Not much," was the reply, "I've only *realized* this umbrella."

This reminds me of a conversation between a man and his wife, which was overheard by the party who repeated it to me. It appears that the lady was economically inclined, and in cutting out some shirts for her husband, resolved that they should not descend much lower than his hips, as thereby so much linen would be saved. The husband expostulated, but in vain. She pointed out to him that it would improve his figure, and make his nether garments set much better; in a word, that long shirt-tails were quite unnecessary; and she wound up her arguments by observing that linen was a very expensive article, and that she could not see what on earth was the reason that people should stuff so much *capital* into their pantaloons.

There is sometimes in the American metaphors an energy which is very remarkable.

"Well, I reckon, that from his teeth to his toe-nail, there's not a human of a more conquering nature than General Jackson."

One *gentleman* said to me, "I wish I had all hell boiled down to a point, just to pour down your throat." . . . .

It is of course not possible for us to deal here with all of the expressions Marryat cited in this selection, but they possess interest for the student of American English. The *um, hu* commented upon approvingly by Marryat is quite common now, and should have long ago found a place in the dictionary but it has not done so.

The verb *raise*, used with reference to people, was adversely commented upon by many of the travelers visiting the United States during the early nineteenth century. Webster in his dictionary of 1828 said that in New England *raise* "is never applied to the breeding of the human race, as it is in the southern states." The writers of grammars and rhetorics have for over a century now voiced their unanimous disapproval of *raise* in the sense pointed out and have commended *rear* for use in connection with "the breeding of the human race." In view of the agitation about *raise* and *rear*, it is surprising to find that a large number of people have never heard of the distinction between these words and have used *raise* with peaceful and pleasurable results in places where, according to the rhetorics, *rear* should have been employed.

The use of *admire* with a following infinitive, as Marryat points out, has, unlike *raise*, not been able to stand up under the bludgeons of its adversaries. One no longer says, "I should admire to go." Webster helped in the stamping-out of this use by not recognizing in his dictionary of 1828 this sense of *admire*, but after defining the word as meaning "to regard with wonder or surprise" he added the comment, "This word has been used in an ill sense, but seems now correctly restricted to the sense here given."

CHAPTER XIII

John Russell Bartlett (1805-86)

JOHN RUSSELL BARTLETT was born in Providence, Rhode Island, and spent most of his life in that place. He was a banker, patron of the arts and sciences, and public official. During his busy life he found time to compile a *Dictionary of Americanisms*, which was published in 1848. In the Introduction to this work there is a section devoted to American dialects, and the first part of that discussion, beginning on page xv, is given below:

Dialects originate in various ways. First, by the proximity of nations speaking different languages, in which case many words and phrases are borrowed from one into the other; witness the Scotch and Irish dialects of the English. Secondly, by migrations. This is the most fruitful and permanent source of dialects. We see its effects in the English language; for the immigration of various nations into Great Britain from the Saxons down to the period of the Norman conquest are yet distinctly marked in the dialects of that country.

In the United States it is easy to point out causes, which, in the course of a few generations, will materially affect the English language in the particular districts of country where those influences are at work. Dialects will spring up as marked as those of Great Britain. A free intercourse may in some cases check the permanency of these dialects; but in those parts of the country aside from the great thoroughfares, where a dialect has once become firmly established, a thousand years will not suffice to eradicate it.

The State of New York was originally settled by the Dutch. The number of their colonists was never large, nor did they extend their settlements beyond the valley of the Mohawk and lands adjacent; yet we find even in this thickly settled State, after a lapse of two hundred years, that they have left evident traces on our spoken language. In the cities of New York and Albany many Dutch words have become incorporated into the common speech. In some of the inland villages of Dutch origin, the inhabitants still use the language of their fathers; and there are even individuals who never spoke any other.

The words so adopted by us embrace geographical names,— a class of words which the first colonists of a country or the primitive inhabitants themselves generally leave to their poster- ity or to the subsequent occupants. Many of the other words which the Dutch have left us are terms belonging to the kitchen. These have been preserved and handed down by cooks and domestic servants, until from constant use they are become familiar to all. Among these terms are *cooky*, *crullers*, *olykoke*, *spack and applejees*, *rullichies*, *kohlslaa*, *pit*.

The terms for various playthings, holidays, &c., preserve among children their original Dutch names; as *scup*, *hoople*, *peewee*, *pile*, *pinkster*, *paas*. Other words confined to children are *pinky*, *terawchy*.

Articles of wearing apparel in some instances retain their Dutch names; as *clockmutch*.

Besides these there are terms the use of which is not confined to the districts originally colonized from Holland, but has been extended to New England and several of the Northern States; such as *stoop*, a porch, *boss*, a master-workman.

If a few Dutch colonists mingled with the English have been able to engraft so many words on our language, what may we expect from the hundreds of thousands of Germans in the State of Pennsylvania? There the German language will doubtless exist for centuries; for, although they are situated in the midst of an English-speaking population far more numerous than themselves, and although the government and laws are con- ducted through the English language, still the tendency of a people of common origin to cling together,—the publication of newspapers, almanacs, and books in German,—and the cultiva- tion to some extent of German literature, will tend to preserve the idiom and nationality of the people. It is true the language is already much corrupted, and in the course of time it must give way to the English; but it will leave behind it an almost imperishable dialect as a memento of its existence. In the State of Ohio, where there are large settlements of Germans, a similar result must follow.

In the State of Illinois is a colony of Norwegians. These people before coming to America sent out an agent, who selected and purchased for them a large tract of land in one section of that State. They were accompanied by their clergyman and schoolmaster. They are thus kept together, and will for a long time preserve their language and nationality. But it must also eventually give way, after engrafting on the English language in that vicinity a Norwegian dialect.

There are large settlements of Welsh emigrants in the States of Pennsylvania and New York. In the latter, in Oneida county, one may travel for miles and hear nothing but the Welsh language. They have their newspapers and magazines in their native tongue, and support many churches wherein their language alone is preached. The Welsh, however, are not in sufficient numbers, nor are they sufficiently isolated to retain for any length of time their native tongue; neither can they produce any sensible dialectical change in our language, owing to the great difference between it and their own. They will, however, add some words to it.

In the State of Louisiana, which was colonized by the French, and Florida, which was colonized by the Spaniards, there are many words of foreign origin, scarcely known in the Northern States. The geographical divisions, the names of rivers, mountains, bays; the peculiarities of soil and climate; all that relates to the cultivation of the earth, the names of fishes, birds, fruits, vegetables, coins, &c., &c., retain to a great extent the names given them by the first possessors of the country. The same class of words is preserved in Lower Canada, where they were originally given by the French. They are now adopted by the English, and will for ever remain in use. Among the words of French origin are *cache, calaboose, bodette, bayou, sault, levee, crevasse, habitan, charivari.*

The Spanish colonists in Florida, and our intercourse with

Mexico and the Spanish main, have been the means of introducing a few Spanish words. Among these are *canyon, cavortin,
chaparral, pistareen, rancho, vamos.*

The Indian terms in our language, as might be supposed, are
numerous. First, as to geographical names. These abound in
every State in the Union, though more in some States than
in others. In New England, particularly on the coast, Indian
names are very common. Nearly all the rivers, bays, and prominent landmarks bear them, as *Housatonic, Connecticut, Quinne-
baug, Pawcatuck, Merrimack, Kennebec, Penobscot, Narraganset,
Passamaquoddy,* &c. In other parts of the country too the
rivers retain their aboriginal names, as the *Mississippi, Ohio,
Susquehanna, Roanoake, Altamaha, Chattahoochie, Alabama,* &c.,
&c. And the same may be said of the great lakes, nearly all the
bays, mountains, and numerous geographical divisions and
localities. Many of the aboriginal names, however, have been
discarded for others less appropriate. In New England the towns
and villages were chiefly named after the towns in England from
which the early colonists emigrated. In the State of New York
there is a strange anomaly in the names of places. Before the
Revolution the people seemed to prefer the aboriginal names;
not only the rivers, lakes, hills, &c., but many of the towns
received them. After the war, the names of distinguished statesmen and soldiers were applied to the new counties and towns.

The greatest perversions of the English language arise from
two opposite causes. One of them is the introduction of vulgarisms by uneducated people, who not having the command of
proper words to express their ideas, invent others for the purpose. These words continue among this class, are transmitted by
them to their children, and thus become permanent and provincial. They are next seized upon by stump-speakers at political meetings, because they have an influence and are popular
with the masses. Next we hear them on the floor of Congress
and in our halls of legislation. Quoted by the newspapers, they
become familiar to all, and take their place in the colloquial language of the whole people. Lexicographers now secure them and
give them a place in their dictionaries; and thus they become
firmly engrafted on our language. The study of lexicography

will show that this process has long been going on in England, and doubtless other languages are subject to similar influences.

But the greatest injury to our language arises from the perversion of legitimate words and the invention of hybrid and other inadmissible expressions by educated men, and particularly by the clergy. This class is the one, above all others, which ought to be the conservators rather than the pervertors of language. It is nevertheless a fact which cannot be denied, that many strange and barbarous words to which our ears are gradually becoming familiar, owe to them their origin and introduction; among them may be mentioned such verbs as to *fellowship*, to *difficult*, to *eventuate*, to *doxologize*, to *happify*, to *donate*, &c., &c.

Political writers have made and are constantly making large additions to our stock of words and phrases. Alex. Hamilton's writings abound in newly coined expressions; many of which have been adopted by Dr. Webster, and have a place in his dictionary. But few, however, have come into general use, as his writings have not been widely diffused, and there is nothing to recommend them for adoption by scholars. Judge Story has contributed his share of new words; but as they are confined to legal treatises and works on the Constitution, they can never seriously affect the language.

Writers of political articles in the newspapers, stump-orators, and the members of legislative bodies, have added much to the English vocabulary. This class of words, though not remarkable for their elegance, are often expressive and become more widely known than other classes. In many instances, however, their existence is but short. They often spring up with a party; and as the parties become extinct, or give place to new ones, the terms which express their peculiar ideas or doctrines likewise fall out of use. In this class may be included such terms as *Old Hunker*, *Bucktail*, *Federalist*, *Barnburner*, *Loco-foco*, *Young Democracy*, *Democratic Republican*, *Native American*, *Nullifier*, *Nullification*, *Coon*, *Coonery*, &c.

There are words, however, in this class, whose origin has grown out of our peculiar institutions, and which consequently are of a permanent nature. The origin of some of these is involved in obscurity, while that of others is well known. Sometimes a little incident trivial in itself has brought into existence words which are extremely expressive, and which will remain as long as our institutions exist. In this class we find *Caucus*, *Buncombe or Bunkum*, *Congress*, to *Lobby*, *Mileage*, *Gubernatorial*, *General Court*, *General Assembly*, President's and Governor's *Messages*, *Senatorial*, &c., &c.

The peculiar physical features of the country—its animals, productions, aborigines, forest life, &c.—have been a most fruitful source, from which has sprung perhaps the largest number of new words, as necessary and useful to ourselves as any derived from our Saxon ancestors. These terms are not used in England, for the simple reason that there they are not wanted. Although I cannot agree with Dr. Webster, that "we rarely find a new word introduced into a language which is entirely useless,"— for there are unquestionably thousands of words encumbering our dictionaries which might well be dispensed with,—yet there is no doubt that, in most instances, "the use of new terms is dictated by necessity or utility; sometimes to express shades of difference in signification, for which the language did not supply a suitable term; sometimes to express a combination of ideas by a single word, which otherwise would require a circumlocution. These benefits, which are often perceived, as it were, instinctively by a nation, recommend such words to common use, till the cavils of critics are silenced by the weight of authority."— *Letter to J. Pickering*, p. 7.

Were we to classify the periods when names were applied to places in the State of New York, for example, we would call that in which the Indian names were applied, the *Aboriginal* period. This is as far back as it would be safe for ordinary mortals to go, leaving the "ante-diluvian" period to the second sight of such seers as Mr. Rafinesque.*

The Indian names seem to have prevailed till the revolution. Then came a burst of patriotism among the settlers, many of whom doubtless had served in the war, and every new place was christened with the names of the warriors and statesmen of the day. Thus arose Washington county, Washington village, and Washington *hollow;* Jefferson county, village, lake, &c. The

* See Introduction to History of Kentucky.

State of New York has thus perpetuated, in her towns and villages, the names of Adams, Jay, La Fayette, Hamilton, Madison, Pinckney, Putnam, Pulaski, Schuyler, De Kalb, Steuben, Sullivan, Gates, Wayne, &c. This may well be styled the *Patriotic* period. But New York appreciated also the military and naval geniuses of other countries, for we find a Nelson, a Moreau, a Waterloo, &c. within her borders. The names of statesmen and generals did not suffice for the patriotism of our early pioneers, for we find interspersed among them the names of Freedom, Freetown, Freeport, Independence, Liberty, Victory, Hopewell, Harmony, Concord, &c.

Next comes the *Classical* period; for by what other term could we designate a period when towns were christened by the names of such men as Homer, Virgil, Solon, Ovid, Cato, Brutus, Pompey, Tully, Cicero, Aurelius, Scipio, Ulysses, Seneca, Hannibal, Hector, Romulus, Lysander, Manlius, Camillus, and Marcellus; or of such places as Athens, Sparta, Troy, Corinth, Pharsalia, Palmyra, Utica, Smyrna, Rome, and Carthage.

Testimony to the piety (to say nothing of the good taste) of our forefathers is also afforded by the occurrence of such names as Eden, Babylon, Sodom, Jerusalem, Jericho, Hebron, Goshen, Bethany, Bethpage, Bethlehem, Sharon, &c. There are towns named after nearly every country in Europe, as Norway, Sweden, Denmark (with a Copenhagen adjoining), Russia, Greece, Italy, Sardinia, Holland, Wales, as well as after their principal cities. There is a town of Mexico, Canton, Peru, Delhi, Cairo, China, Cuba. Distinguished men in English history, as Milton, Addison, Dryden, Scott, Byron, Chesterfield, Marlborough, Junius, have towns christened with their names. But little fondness is exhibited for dramatic authors, as the name of the greatest of them all has been forgotten. Not even a pond, a hollow, or a swamp has been honored with the name of Shakspeare. If we were to classify all the names of places in the State of New York, we should be puzzled for a place to put the names of Painted Post, Oxbow, Halfmoon, Owl Pond, Oyster Bay, Mud Creek, Cow Neck, Mosquito Cove, and the like. The name of *Pennyan* is said to have been manufactured by the first settlers, part of whom were from Pennsylvania and the rest from New

England, by taking the first syllable from "Pennsylvania," and the last from "Yankee."

Now the Mexican war is over, we shall doubtless have a large fund of names to use in our newly acquired territories, and the new States at the West. The old generals of the revolution will be passed by, and the span-new heroes of this war will be handed down to the admiration of posterity in the metamorphosed shape of cities, towns, and villages, yet to come into existence. As the simplicity of the revolutionary period no longer remains, the plain surname will not answer now-a-days; but the love of glory and the love of magniloquence may both be gratified in such euphonious compounds as Quitmanville, Pillowtown, and *Polkopolis!*

The class of words which owe their origin to circumstances or productions peculiar to the United States, such as *backwoods, backwoodsmen, breadstuffs, barrens, bottoms, buffalo-robe, canebrake, cypress-brake, clapboard, corn broom, corn-shucking, clearing, deadening, diggings, dug-out, flat boat, husking, pine barrens, prairie, prairie dog, prairie hen, shingle, sawyer, salt lick, savannah, snag, sleigh,* &c., are necessary additions to the language.

The metaphorical and other odd expressions used first at the West, and afterwards in other parts of the country, often originate in some curious anecdote or event, which is transmitted from mouth to mouth, and soon made the property of all. Political writers and stump speakers perform a prominent part in the invention and diffusion of these phrases. Among these may be mentioned, *to cave in, to acknowledge the corn, to flash in the pan, to bark up the wrong tree, to pull up stakes, to be a caution, to fizzle out, to flat out, to fix his flint, to be among the missing, to give him Jessy, to see the elephant, to fly around, to tucker out, to use up, to walk into, to mizzle, to absquatulate, to cotton, to hifer,* &c., &c.

Our people, particularly those who belong to the West and South, are fond of using intensive and extravagant epithets, both as adjectives and adverbs, as *awful, powerful, monstrous, dreadful, mighty, almighty, all-fired,* &c.

The words *bankable, boatable, mailable, mileage,* are well formed and useful terms which have been generally adopted by those who have occasion to make use of them. But the words *dubersome, disremember, decedent, docity,* cannot be called useful or necessary additions to our language.

The Indian element in our language, or rather the Indian words which have become adopted in it, consist, 1st. Of geographical names. 2d. Of the names of various animals, birds, and fishes. 3d. Of fruits and cereals; particularly the several preparations of the latter for eating. Thus from Indian corn, we have *samp, hominy,* and *supawn;* from the manioc plant, *mandioca* and *tapioca.* 4th. Such articles known to and used by the Indians, which the Europeans did not possess, as *canoe, hammock, tobacco, moccasin, pemmican;* also, *barbecue, hurricane, pow-wow.*

The Indian names of animals, fishes, and reptiles, are generally local. Thus a fish may be known by different names in Boston, New York, and Delaware Bay, as *scup, paugie,* and *scuppaug.*

There is a diversity in the pronunciation of certain words in different parts of the United States, which is so perceptible that a native of these particular districts may be at once recognised by a person who is observant in these matters. Residents of the city of New York are, perhaps, less marked in their pronunciation and use of words, than the residents of any other city or State, the reason of which is obvious. The population is so fluctuating, so many people from every part of the country, as well as from England, Scotland, and Ireland, are congregated here, who are in daily contact with each other, that there is less chance for any idiom or peculiarity of speech to grow up. The large number of educated men in New England, her admirable schools and higher institutions of education, have had a powerful influence in moulding the language of her people. Yet, notwithstanding this fact, in Boston and other towns in Massachusetts, there exist some glaring errors in the vulgar speech. There are peculiarities also to be observed in the literary language of the Bostonians. The great extent to which the scholars of New England have carried the study of the German language and literature for some years back, added to a very general neglect of the old masterpieces of English composition, have had the effect of giving to the writings of many of them an artificial, unidiomatic character, which has an inexpressibly unpleasant effect to those who are not habituated to it.

The agricultural population who live in the interior of New England, have a strongly marked provincial dialect, by which they may be distinguished from the people of every other part of the Union. The chief peculiarity is a drawling pronunciation, sometimes accompanied by a speaking through the nose, as *eend* for *end*, *dawg* for *dog*, *Gawd* for *God*, &c. Before the sounds *ow* and *oo*, they often insert a short *i*, which we will represent by the letter *y; as kyow* for *cow*, *vyow* for *vow*, *tyoo* for *too*, *dyoo* for *do*, &c. &c.

The numerous words employed in New England, which are not heard in other parts of the country, are mostly genuine old words still provincial in the North of England; very few are of indigenous origin.

The chief peculiarity in the pronunciation of the Southern and Western people is the giving of a broader sound than is proper to certain vowels; as *whar* for *where*, *thar* for *there*, *bar* for *bear*.

CHAPTER XIV

Southwestern Vernacular

WE CONCLUDE our selections with an article which appeared under the title "South-western Slang" in the August, 1869, number of the *Overland Monthly*, III, 125–31. If Socrates Hyacinth, as the writer of this contribution was styled, had really confined his article to slang, it would not be of interest to us here. An examination of it shows that a fair number of the terms dealt with are not slang, but interesting words that may be termed "westernisms."

SOUTH-WESTERN SLANG

It may be doubted if there is any other State in the Union which pretends to rival Texas in the startling originality of its slang.

In his category of persons who are "of imagination all compact," Shakspeare assigns the first place to the lunatic, above the lover and the poet. There are persons so artless as to believe that this was done simply in obedience to the necessities of the verse; but such have only once to become familiar with the vernacular of Texas to perceive that, in this matter, as in every other which he touched, Shakspeare was right, as if by intuition. Nature herself, elsewhere a dame so staid and so proper, there gives much reason for the issuance of a writ *de lunatico inquirendo*. The rabbits have somehow gotten the body of the hare and the ears of the ass; the frogs, the body of the toad, the horns of the stag-beetle, and the tail of the lizard; the trees fall up-hill, and the lightning comes out of the ground. In such a country it is not to be wondered at that their sesquipedalian adjectives get somewhat twisted in coming up out of the hard, waxy prairies. In short, Texas is one great, windy lunatic; or, if you please, a bundle of crooked and stupendous phrases, tied together with a thong of rawhide.

As a specimen of Texan ingenuity, or rather perverseness of imagination, take its code of morals, which is embraced in two sayings. The first is, "Revolvers make all men equal;" and the second is the famous utterance of Houston, "If a man can't curse his friends, whom can he curse?"

But it is in geography that this gift gives forth its most amazing manifestations. We all have heard some of our exquisite American names, such as Last Chance, Sorrel Horse, Righteous Ridge, Scratch Gravel, Pinchtown, Marrow Bones, etc.; but now read these from Texas: Lick Skillet, Buck Snort, Nip and Tuck, Jimtown, Rake Pocket, Hog Eye, Fair Play, Seven League, Steal Easy, Possum Trot, Flat Heel, Frog Level, Short Pone, Gourd Neck, Shake Rag, Poverty Slant, Black Ankle, Jim Ned.

Next after such slops and parings of names as these, Texas is notable for the number of its obscure personal names, tortured into the service of municipal nomenclature. These, together with a certain absurd classical Grub-street vocabulary, make our atlases contemptible, and an object of deserved ridicule for foreigners. The preponderance of these personal names in the South, especially in Texas, is probably to be explained in this manner: Smith owned a great plantation here; Jones, another adjoining; and between their houses, which were miles apart, nobody resided, since those who would have occupied the interval in the North were all grouped about the two mansions as slaves. In these little colonies there frequently grew up smithies, groceries, etc.; and travelers found it convenient to designate distances on the road as so far to Smith's, or so far from Jones', which presently crystallized into Smithville and Jonesborough. In the North the land was divided more equally among the people, and as none was prominent enough to aspire to the honors of geography, they gratified their collective quadrivial ambition with Rome, or something else. Athens, Jonesville, Winnipiseogee, Pig Misery!

In the course of a rather leisurely walk through Texas, and then across the continent with a company of emigrants, I noted a large number of curious words, names, and phrases not found in the current collections of Americanisms, a large moiety of which are indigenous to Texas; and they are herewith set forth, without any thing more than the most superficial attempt to make out their etyma.

Among names of revolvers I remember the following: Meat in the Pot, Blue Lightning, Peacemaker, Mr. Speaker, Black-eyed Susan, Pill-box, My Unconverted Friend.

The occupation of the Texans as cattle-breeders has given rise to a great number of new words, and new uses of old words. To illustrate: On the Trinity prairies I met a man, with a pinched face and a yellow beard, who was mounted on a clay-bank horse as lank as a Green Mountain pad when it has been about a month in the Horse Latitudes, and so sway-backed that the rider's feet nearly dragged on the prairie. Yet it held up its pikestaff neck so high that a line drawn across from the top of its head over the rider's head would have touched its little stump tail, which stood up like an ear of corn. He had a long coil of *cabestros* dangling from the pommel of his saddle, and was evidently in search of strays, for he asked me if I had seen a red mulley cow, with a crop and an underbit in the right and a marked crop in the left. I told him I had not; but that I had seen a brown-and-white-pied calf, with an overslope and a slit in the right, and a swallow-fork in the left; also, a black-and-white-paint horse, fifteen hands high, and an old gray mare, considerably flea-bitten, with a blazed face and a docked tail. He smiled faintly, and rode away.

Perhaps the only interpretation here needed is, that in Texas "mulley" always means *hornless;* that a "flea-bitten" color is one dotted with minute specks of white and black, like pepper and salt; and that "clay-bank" is a yellowish dun.

The brands of Texas and their descriptive names would fill all the books of the Nuremberg Cobbler. Indeed, the State is one great tangle of bovine hieroglyphics, which the Texans read better than a book; but which I could no more make out than Mr. Pickwick could the sign-manual of Bill Stubbs. If, however, a Texan's reading is occasionally contested, he has a one-eyed scribe, who is more infallible, as a last resort, than any Vatican manuscript.

On the march the mighty herd sometimes strings out miles

in length, and then it has "pointers," who ride abreast of the head of the column, and "siders," who keep the stragglers out of the chaparral. At night they "round up" or "corral" ("corral," in Texas, means also to herd without an inclosure, on the open prairie). The various reliefs during the day and night speak of being "on herd" or "off herd," very much as if they were performing military duty. It often happens, in a populated country—when they are honest drovers—that they are obliged to stop and "stray" the herd. While several herdsmen are stationed around it to hold it fast, another rides in, selects a stray brand, and "cuts it out," by chasing it out with his horse. At other times they "bear off" a single animal, by riding between it and the herd, when in motion. Sometimes, too, when they have made a march through a dense chaparral, they halt, go back, and "drive" it, by riding systematically through it, in search of stragglers. Two men often "bunch" on the march, *i.e.*, unite their herds for convenience in driving.

The statute of Texas once was, (and may yet be) that all cattle which were allowed to pass the age of one year unbranded became the property of him whose brand was first put upon them. One Maverick formerly owned such immense herds that many of his animals unavoidably escaped his rouanne in the spring, were taken up by his neighbors, branded and called "mavericks." The term eventually spread over the whole State, and is in use now, not only to denote a waif thus acquired, but any young animal. No great drove can sweep through this mighty unfenced State without drawing a wake of these "mavericks"—these *boves per dolum amotas*—and the temptations to let them remain has ruined the herdsman's character. Go to Texas and begin to speak of an honest drover, and you shall be rewarded with a smile.

With the Texan driver all oxen are "steers," and he has his "wheel-steers," his "swing-steers," and his "lead-steers." He never uses the former word in the singular, and very seldom in the plural, when it is almost invariably "oxens." He never says to oxen, "gee," but "back;" never "haw," but "whoa, come." The "cow-whip" is a very long lash with a very short stock, and is used only in driving the herd, which is often called "the cows;"

but the "ox-whip" has both parts as long as they can be man-
aged. I have seen a poor fellow from Ohio, totally unused to this
enormous affair, swing it around his head in many an awkward
twirl, while the Texans stood by and laughed to see him knock
off his hat and "bat" his eyes at every twitch, to avoid cutting
them out. [Cf. Italian, *batter d'occhio*—twinkling of an eye.]

After a long desert journey the oxen become much "petered;"
indeed, I may say they become altogether "petered." Hence,
on the first good grass which they "strike" they halt a few days,
and allow the teams to graze undisturbed, which makes them
"all a-setting" again. They have queer names for their oxen.
In the North each farmer owns a single yoke, and from Maine
to Indiana they have pretty much the same names; but in Texas
many men own many yoke, and you might fill a book with their
grotesque names, such as Presbyterian and Methodist, Rock and
Brandy, Benjamin and Filibuster.

Toward the last, when the teams are terribly thinned out,
and their poor old bones lie all along the road quite back to Texas,
then the emigrants begin to yoke in the cows. Like women, they
are the "contrariest" things in creation to manage. They run
like the wind, then jump right up and down, and shake their
heads, and twist themselves in a manner which is wonderful to
behold. Sometimes an infuriated old mulley gets loose, and
chases a man for rods, with her horns just missing an important
portion of his trowsers at every plunge. After an incredible
amount of pulling and "jiggering" about, they are gotten into
the team, and then comes the driver's turn, and the refractory
Nancy and Susan are severely fustigated.

For horses they used still another kind of whip, the "quirt"
[from the Spanish]. A trig, smirk little horse is a "lace-horse,"
and he often has to "june," or "quill," or "get up and quill," or
"get up and dust." [There is a large colony of Germans in Western Texas, and "june" is said to be corrupted from their *gehen*.]
All over the South they feed a horse "roughness," (any kind of
fodder, as distinguished from grain) but in Texas they "stake
him out," and he gets nothing else but "roughness." I have even
heard a Texan speak of land which he had "lariated out," meaning thereby that he had just bought it from Government, but not

occupied it yet. It is amusing to hear one ask of another, when about to purchase a horse: "Is he religious?" Query: Do they have in mind the Egyptian *Ibis religiosa?* A mustang is generally any thing in the world but "religious," for he will both "sull," (have the sulks) and "buck." This latter operation consists in plunging forward, and throwing the head to the ground, in an effort to unseat the rider—a motion of which probably no domesticated beast is capable, aside from this miserable and treacherous species of horse. In fact, a mustang is not "worth shucks." He will run "skygodlin" (obliquely); lie down and roll over; then "get up and scallyhoot" a short distance; then stop so "suddent," and "rare up" behind, that the rider continues his travels a little distance on his own account, and alights upon his pate. [With "scallyhoot" cf. *scat, scateran;* and Welsh *hwt,* hoot.] Several persons in our "lay-out" (*i.e.,* our company) in New Mexico "swapped" good American horses for mustangs, for some little boot of onions or "sech like truck," and made about as good bargains as Moses Primrose did when he exchanged a horse for a lot of old green spectacles.

In addition to the usual methods of hoppling a horse, the Texans often "side-line" him, by tying a fore to a hind leg. "Better count ribs than tracks," is a proverbial expression of caution which may be heard on the frontiers, and which originated from this practice of picketing animals. When a horse is kept thus close for a long time, "his bones, that were not seen, stick out," but this is considered better than to have him stolen, and be obliged to go in pursuit.

The war originated a great many new phrases in the imaginative South—far more, if they were all recorded, than in the North. "Cousin Sal" is pretty generally lamented throughout the South as the deceased and only daughter of our very worthy and revered "Uncle Sam"—the same having been begotten by him in the bonds of lawful wedlock with "Aunty Extension." You may hear the word "Confederate" singularly used. For instance, when a Texan wishes to express the strongest possible approval of some sentiment, he will exclaim, "You're mighty Confederate!" The Rebels had their "bluebacks" for money; but in Texas, where they have always clung tenaciously to their silver, they made slow progress, and were received with much reluctance. $100 bills were there called "Williams," and $50 bills "Blue Williams." Nevertheless, a Texan once told me, with a fierce glitter of satisfaction in his eye, that "he had $100,000 in 'Williams' laid up against that day, which was certain to come, when he could exchange it, dollar with dollar, for greenbacks." The poor fellow! I should much prefer a draft for ten cents on the Old Lady of California street. Neither did greenbacks succeed well at first in invading the State. In March, 1868, they had gotten no farther west than Marshall, and everywhere west of that, when a man named a price, he meant "spizerinctums" (corrupted from *specie*).

The fierce military spirit of the South is shown in the scorn and contempt which they heaped on men who refused to go out to battle. In Texas they were called, with a play on the word *women*, (in the South often pronounced *weemen*) and a hint at their former gasconade as to what "we" could do—"we-men." Some boasted that one Southerner could "whale" ten Yankees. Lieutenant J. W. Boothe, of the Seventh Texas Battalion, I am told, first applied to this sort the phrase "ten-strikers," which became immensely popular in that State. In the cis-Mississippi States they were generally dubbed "bomb-proofs."

A story is related of a brigade of North Carolinians, who, in one of the great battles, (Chancellorsville, if I remember correctly) failed to hold a certain hill, and were laughed at by the Mississippians for having forgotten to tar their heels that morning. Hence originated their cant name, "Tar-heels."

For a very obvious reason, the South Carolinians are called "Rice-birds." Wherever in the South you see a man take boiled rice on his plate and eat it heartily without condiments, you may know he is a South Carolinian as infallibly as you may that a man is plebeian-bred when he picks his teeth in the horse-car without holding his hand before his mouth. On the other hand, when you see a man, at the traditional hour sacred in New England to mince-pie, get a cold, boiled sweet potato a little smaller than his calf, quarter it length-ways, take a quarter in one hand, and a piece of cane-brake cheese in the other, and eat them by the light of a pine fire, you may be certain he is a North Carolinian.

A Georgian is popularly known in the South as a "Goubergrabbler" ["gouber" for *gopher*, pea-nut—a nut which is exceedingly abundant in that State].

For no particular reason that I am aware of, a Virginian is styled a "Clover-eater."

The cant designation in the Rebel army for a man of Arkansas was "Josh." This is said to have originated in a jocular attempt to compare Arkansas, Texas, and part of Louisiana to the two tribes and a half who had their possessions beyond Jordan, but went over with Joshua to assist the remaining tribes. Just before the battle of Murfreesboro' (the story hath it) the Tennesseans, seeing a regiment from Arkansas approach, cried out, a little confused in their Biblical recollections: "Here come the tribes of Joshua, to fight with their brethren!"

For the Texan soubriquet "Chub" I know of no explanation, unless it be found in the size of the Eastern Texans. It is related of the Fifteenth Texas Infantry, for instance, that at the mustering-in no member was of a lighter weight than a hundred and eighty pounds, while the large number made the scale-beam kick at two hundred.

On account of the great number of gophers in that State, and the former use of their skins for money, a Floridian is called a "Gopher."

This inexhaustible fertility of imagination was occasionally useful to the Rebel soldiers, in enabling them to eke out and variegate their lean commissary. A hog clandestinely killed outside of camp and smuggled in under cover of darkness, was called a "slow bear." Despite their strategy they were often detected, but then, so lax was Confederate discipline, they generally escaped by inviting in their officers to dine off the "bear." "Mud-lark" signified the same thing. In an attempt to vary their everlasting pork and corn-bread, when the latter waxed old, they crumbled it fine and fried it in grease—a mess which they called "cush." Many a Rebel cavalryman has told me that he had often received in the morning, as his day's ration, an ear of corn on the cob, and had sometimes gone forty-eight hours without a "snook" of any thing. When he munched a piece of crust, or any unmoistened provisions, as he sat in his saddle, he was eating his "dry Mike."

Southern smoke-cured pork, in distinction from the Northern

salted article, in allusion to the famous negro song, was termed "Old Ned," from its sable appearance. North Carolinians call skim-milk "blue John." This is entirely gratuitous, and therefore an insult to old mulley, in a land where cream rises as thin as the oil on boarding-house soup. It shows, however, the fondness which the Southerners have for good milk and its corollaries. In no other place in the Union can you find the genuine Irish bonny-clabber, sung by Dean Swift: that is, sour, thick buttermilk. Let it get old, and rich, and a little turned, then take selected, red sweet potatoes, and steam them moist and treacle-like, and you have the best eating in thirty-seven States. My memory waters in the mouth while I write thereof.

In most of the Atlantic Southern States there is a dish to be found about hog-slaughtering time, named "puddings." It consists of swine's flesh, bread, sage, and other matters of nourishment and seasoning, chopped fine, and then squirted out into links from the end of a sausage-gun. It is well worth eating, when neatly prepared. Then there are the delusive "kettlings," among the "low-down" people. Not to harrow the reader's stomach by a minute description, I will simply say that it is fried sausages, minus all the unhealthy and absurd meat which most people insist on stuffing into the intestinal integuments. "Collard" [probably corrupted from *colewort*] is the kind of cabbage found everywhere in the South, whose leaves, not heads, furnish the greens for the inevitable dish of bacon and greens. The word is so common that it is singular it has not found its way into the dictionaries. "Pinetop" is a kind of mean turpentine whisky of North Carolina.

As for diseases, "Bronze John" is pretty well known for yellow fever. It is amusing to hear the people of the South speak in such a matter-of-fact way of fever and ague as their regular occupation: "Jones, are you chilling it much this winter?" "Well, (chatter—chatter) Smith, (shiver—chatter) right (chatter—shiver—chatter) smart." Of course, this only happens in "chilly" countries. Then in Texas they have the "higulcion flips," which is what the French would call a sort of *maladie sans maladie;* about equivalent, perhaps, to our "conniption fits," which the ladies can best define.

Of terms used by agriculturists there are several not recorded.

Planters everywhere in the South say they have a good "stand," when the corn or cotton plants come up thick enough in the rows to insure an ordinary harvest; and in that case, if the cotton or other worms do not molest them, they will "make" a good crop. Texas is notable for the number of its soils. In Montgomery County there is what they call a "peach-bud." Then there is the "chocolate" prairie, and the "mulatto," and the "mezquite," (producing chiefly mezquite, both bush and grass) and the "hummock," (yielding principally small honey-locusts) and the "wire-grass." A "tank" in Texas is a pond of fresh water, and a "swag" is a kind of hollow which seems to be peculiar to its prairies—narrow, shallow, and marshy and rush-grown at the bottom.

When a Texan driver wishes to mend any part of his wagon underneath, he often has to "cut" it, *i.e.*, throw the fore wheels out of alignment with the others.

But the Rawhide State particularly excels in that fusty savagery of idioms peculiar to the swaggering drawcansirs of the South-west. When two roughs fall to quarreling about any matter, one of them usually administers to the other some species of a "snifter," or, more commonly, "curries him down with a six-shooter." When he wishes to express a peculiarly fierce and inexorable resolve, he avows his dreadful purpose to be "essentially jumped-up" before he will permit such or such a thing; or "dog my cats if you shall," or "dad-snatched if you can." When one of the fellows is a "gyascutus," and the other is a "kiamuck," you may look for some rare sport. You need apprehend nothing dreadful, for boobies seldom "John Brown" each other. Neither of them will, like De Quincey's unfortunate Aroar, fall into an "almighty fix," though he may get into a "dog-oned fixment;" or he may, in a very extreme case, become seriously "golum-gumptiated." [Since this word means *befooled* or *obfuscated*, it is possible that it is compounded of *gull* and *gumption*.] "To have the drop on," *i.e.*, to have the advantage of, appears to refer to a cowardly state of things. The figure presented is that of one man prostrate under another, who is about to drop some jagged piece of stone or wood which may impinge upon and bruise his eyes.

If there be one thing more than another which disgusted a Northern man in the South, it is the fondness which they had for speculating as to the fate of Booth. In certain circles in Texas a young rough had no more certain means of raising a laugh than to ejaculate, at every absurdest cranny of the conservation, a travesty of his famous (reputed) exclamation—*sic semper tyrannis*—in this shape, "Six serpents and a tarantula."

When a Texan goes forth on a sparking errand, he does not go to pay his devoirs to his Amaryllis, his Lalage, his Dulcinea, or other such antiquated object of affection, but (employing a word worthy of a place in the pasilaly of mankind) his "jimpsecute." She, on the other hand, is said to receive attention from her "juicy-spicy." I knew a man in Texas once who had no more sense than to have a "jimpsecute," and this was all her name: Dionysia Boadicea Jeffalinda Jacobina Christiana Buckiana Caledonia Susannah Emily Wyatt Wilkinson Moore Wynne!

A Texan never has a great quantity of any thing, but he has "scads" of it, or "oodles," or "dead oodles," or "scadoodles," or "swads."

In Texas you never have *things* in your house, or *baggage* on your journey, but "tricks."

"Moke," a negro, (seemingly derived from Icelandic *möckvi*, darkness) is a word chiefly in use among the Regulars stationed in Texas and in the Territories. The word also has Cymric affinities, and was probably brought into currency by Welsh recruits, who have occasionally drifted into the army from New York City.

"Fide on the jeck," for confident on the subject, is a singular instance of the barbarous corruptions of the South-west.

Then there is another phrase, "human scabs," for money; as, "I'd like to strike somebody that I could blister, and raise some human scabs." There is more philosophy than poetry in that phrase, "human scabs."

"Rance sniffle" is a strange combination of words to express a mean and dastardly piece of malignity. I have never heard it outside of Georgia.

In Texas "scringe" means *to flinch*.

Soon is used adjectively all over the South; as, "If I get a soon start in the morning, I'll be thar before sunup."

During the war we all heard enough of "we-uns" and "you-uns," but "you-alls" was to me something fresh.

Some of the expressions contained in this article merit further attention.

Clay-bank and *maverick* are still in good use; the latter expression originated about 1850 in the way pointed out here.

Gouber, usually spelled *goober*, is also in common use in the South. The dictionaries point out that it is of unknown, though possibly of African, origin. Our author associates the word with *gopher*, but in reality they have no connection. Concerning the word *gopher*, the writer later on makes an amusing error when commenting on the use of the word as a nickname for Floridians. The gopher that is plentiful in Florida is a kind of shellbacked land turtle, the skin of which would certainly not make a practical currency.

There is one other place, too, where this writer makes an error. After explaining that a mulley cow is one having no horns he speaks of a mulley that chases a man and of her horns "just missing an important portion of his trowsers."

Cush is still occasionally heard in the South. The preparation of the article of food it designates is not as crude a process as, evidently, it used to be. *Bluejohn*, like *cush*, still survives in dialect use, but it has not made its way into standard speech. *Kettlings* must be used for *chitterlings*, though the *OED* does not record such a variant. *Chitterlings* has been in the language for five or six centuries. The article of food it refers to is esteemed a great delicacy by some people, but others, not to the manner born, find their gastronomic sensibilities greatly upset at the thoughts of partaking of such a dish.

Stand, in the sense specified, is evidently an Americanism. The date of the earliest citation of it in the *OED* is 1868.

Index

broke, *p.p.*, 22
Bronze John, 159
brown meal, 135
brussels, 58
buck, 156
Bucktail, 145
buffalo-robe, 148
bug, 8, 102
bunch, 154
buncombe, bunkum, 146
burnt brandy, 115
buty, 58, 62
by, 77, 89

cabestros, 153
cache, 103, 143
calaboose, 143
calculate, 58, 62, 103, 134
calico, 4
campus, 7
cane-brake, 148
canoe, 149
canyon, 144
capersome, 114
capital, 139
capting, 118
captivate, 58, 81
carry, 18, 118, 122
case, 102
catamount, 133
catch up, 103
caucus, 50, 103, 146
caution, to be a, 148
cave in, 148
cavort, 95, 96, 103, 114, 144
cawker, 104
cent, 58, 103
centrality, 103
certain, 19
chaffering, 58
chance, 103, 121
chaparral, 144

chare, 58
charivari, 143
charot, 118
charrackter, 118
chaunce, 58
check, 135
checkers, chequers, 103
cheer, 90, 118
chicken fixings, 135
chimbly, 118
chimpanzee, 4
chinch, 8
chinquapin, 2
chirk, 58, 62
chocolate, 160
choosed, 118
chore, 58
christiun, 118
Chub, 158
chunk, 25, 32, 118
churk, 58
cigar, 48
circumsurround, 114
citess, 81
clamjamphrie, 114
clapboard, 148
clay-bank, 153, 162
clear out, 137
clearing, 148
clerk, 36, 124
clever, 19, 32, 36, 37, 58, 103
cleverly, 58, 62
clitchy, 76
cloak, 36, 37
clockmutch, 142
clodpolish, 114
close, 58
clothier, 103
clover-eater, 158
clus, 58
coasting coat, 6
cob, 103

⟦ PRINTED
IN U·S·A ⟧